STAR WARS®

CLONE WARS

ADVENTURES

VOLUME 2

This book
belongs
to Kayla
9ESEI morrow
4th grade

designer
Joshua Elliott

assistant editor
Dave Marshall

editors
Jeremy Barlow
Randy Stradley

publisher
Mike Richardson

special thanks to Sue Rostoni and Amy Gary
at Lucas Licensing

talk about this book online at: *www.darkhorse.com/community/boards*

✦ The events in this story take place approximately
five months after the Battle of Geonosis.

Advertising Sales: (503) 652-8815 x370
Comic Shop Locator Service: (888) 266-4226
www.darkhorse.com
www.starwars.com

STAR WARS®
CLONE WARS
ADVENTURES
VOLUME 2

"SKYWALKERS"
script **Haden Blackman**
Additional dialogue by George Lucas
From *Star Wars:* Episode IV *A New Hope*
art **The Fillbach Brothers**
colors **Wil Glass**

"HIDE IN PLAIN SIGHT"
script **Welles Hartley**
art **The Fillbach Brothers**
colors **SnoCone Studios**

"RUN MACE RUN"
script and art **The Fillbach Brothers**
colors **Wil Glass**

lettering
Michael David Thomas

cover
The Fillbach Brothers and Dan Jackson

Dark Horse Books™

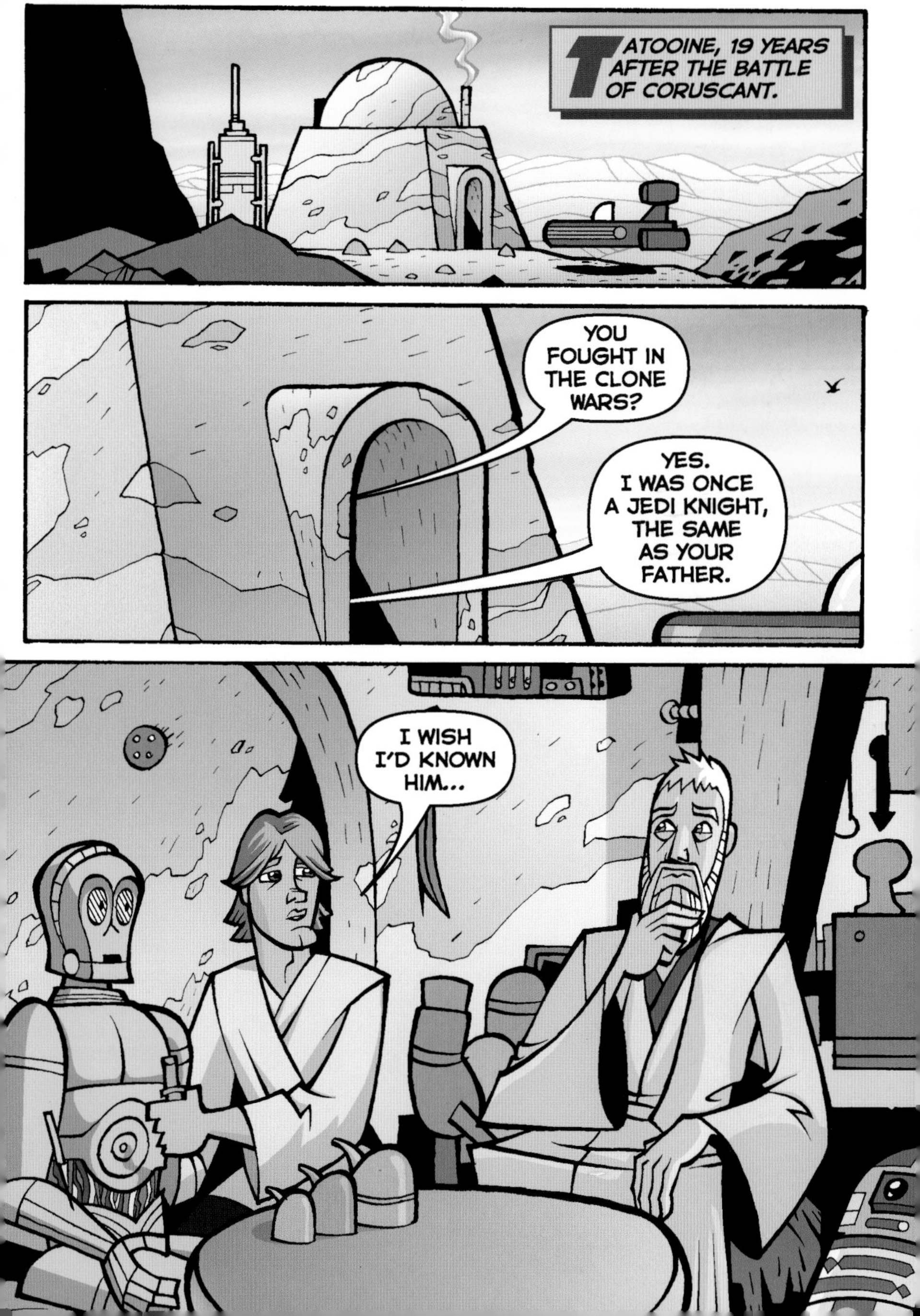
TATOOINE, 19 YEARS AFTER THE BATTLE OF CORUSCANT.
YOU FOUGHT IN THE CLONE WARS?
YES. I WAS ONCE A JEDI KNIGHT, THE SAME AS YOUR FATHER.
I WISH I'D KNOWN HIM...

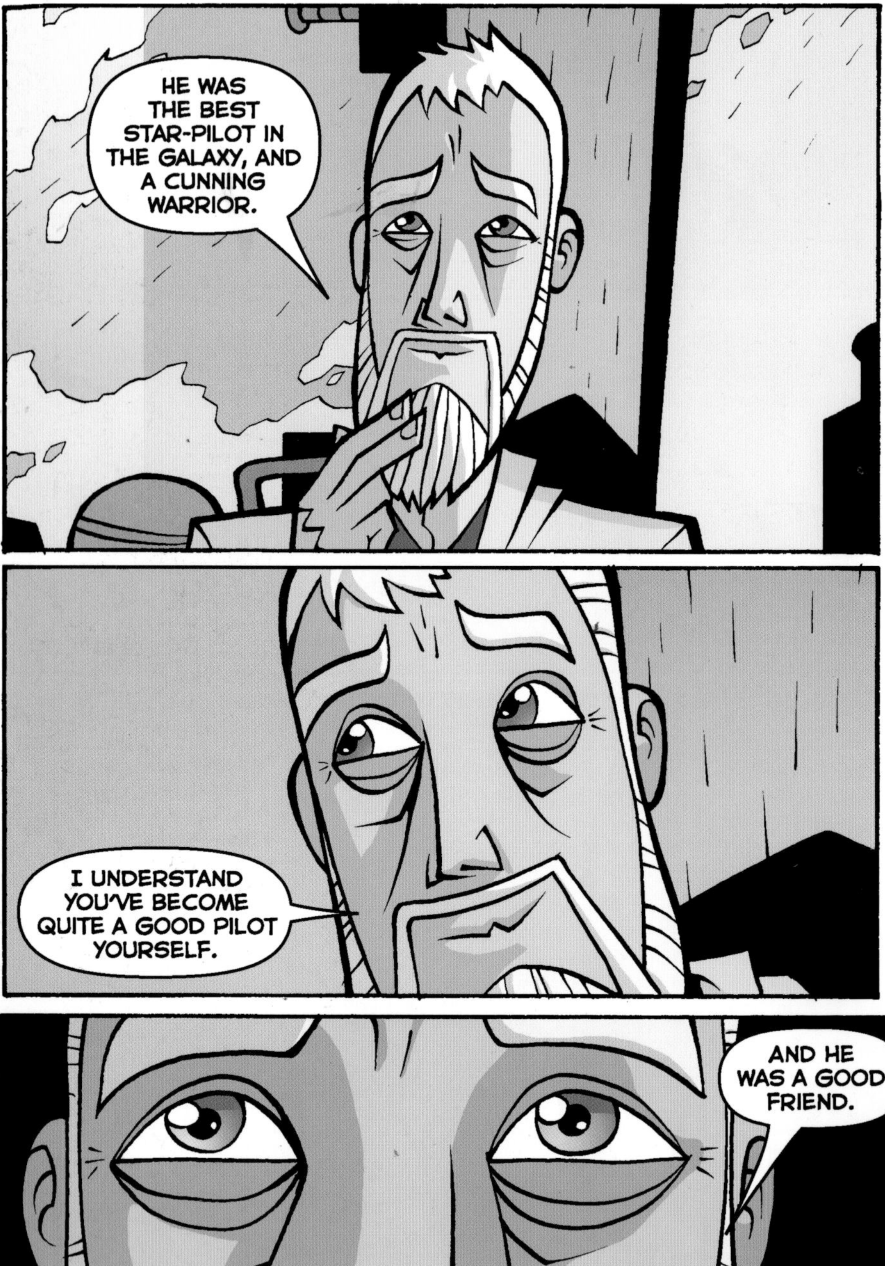
HE WAS THE BEST STAR-PILOT IN THE GALAXY, AND A CUNNING WARRIOR.
I UNDERSTAND YOU'VE BECOME QUITE A GOOD PILOT YOURSELF.
AND HE WAS A GOOD FRIEND.

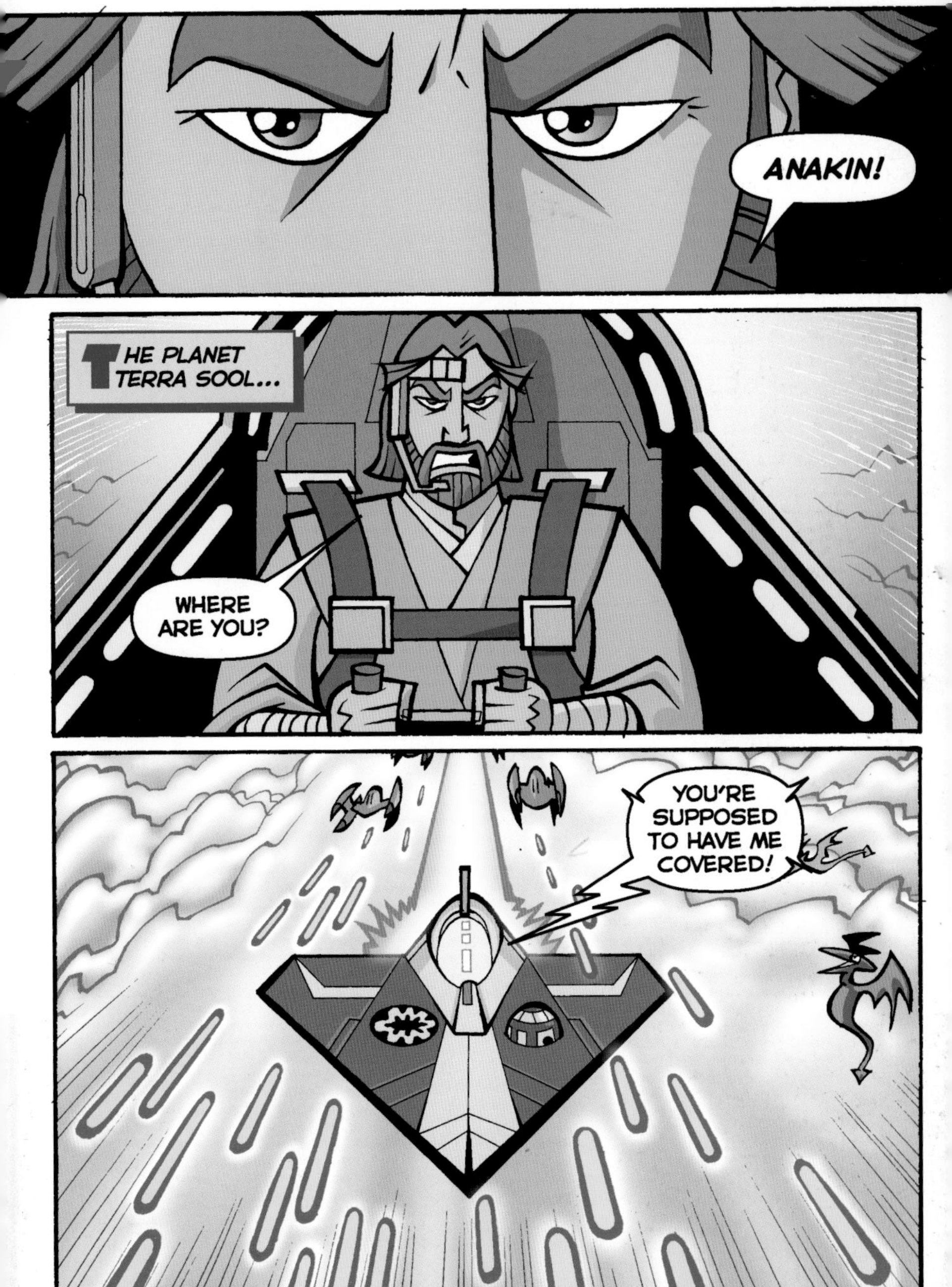
ANAKIN!
THE PLANET TERRA SOOL...
WHERE ARE YOU?
YOU'RE SUPPOSED TO HAVE ME COVERED!

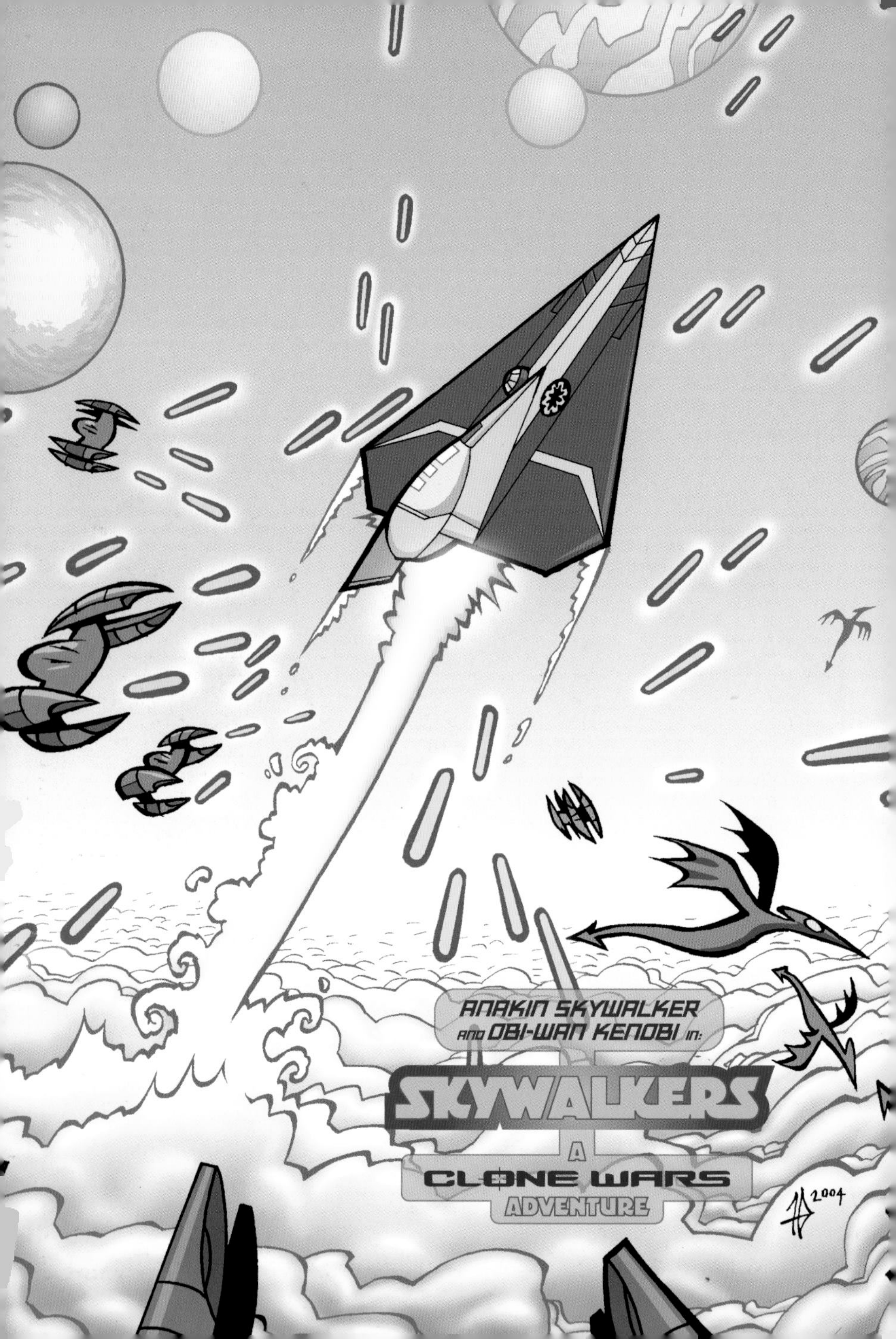
ANAKIN SKYWALKER
AND OBI-WAN KENOBI IN:
SKYWALKERS
A
CLONE WARS
ADVENTURE
2004

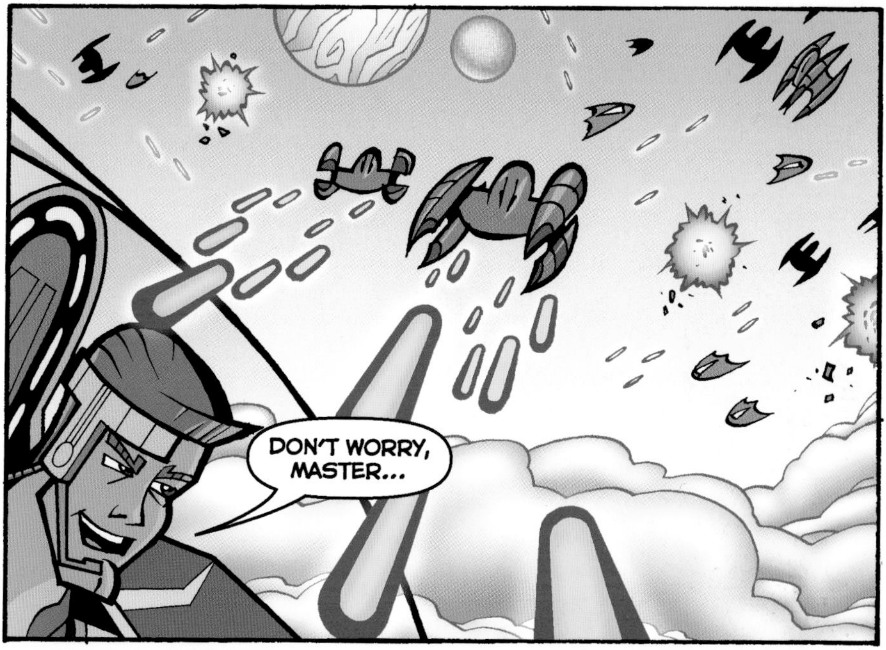
DON'T WORRY, MASTER...

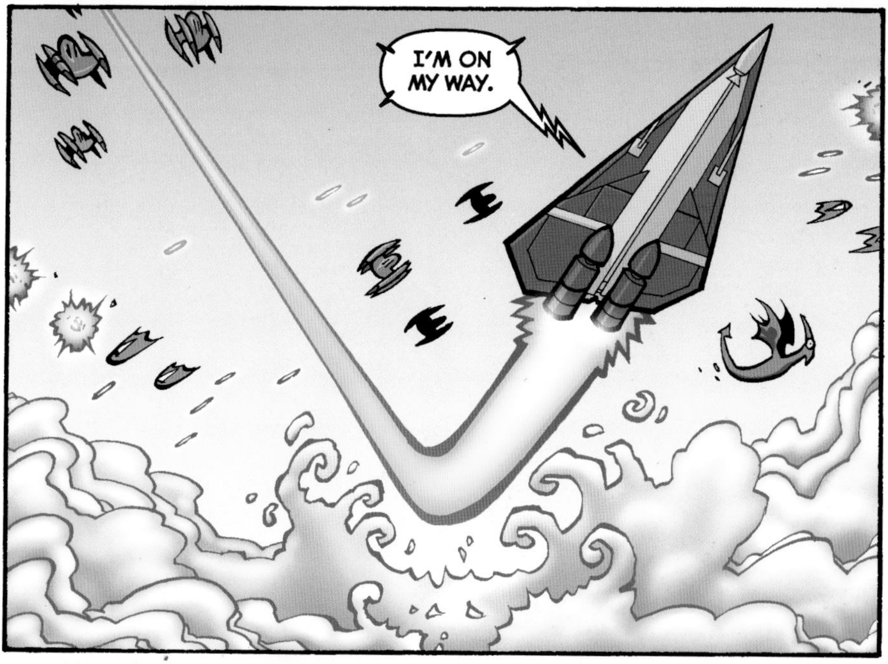
I'M ON MY WAY.

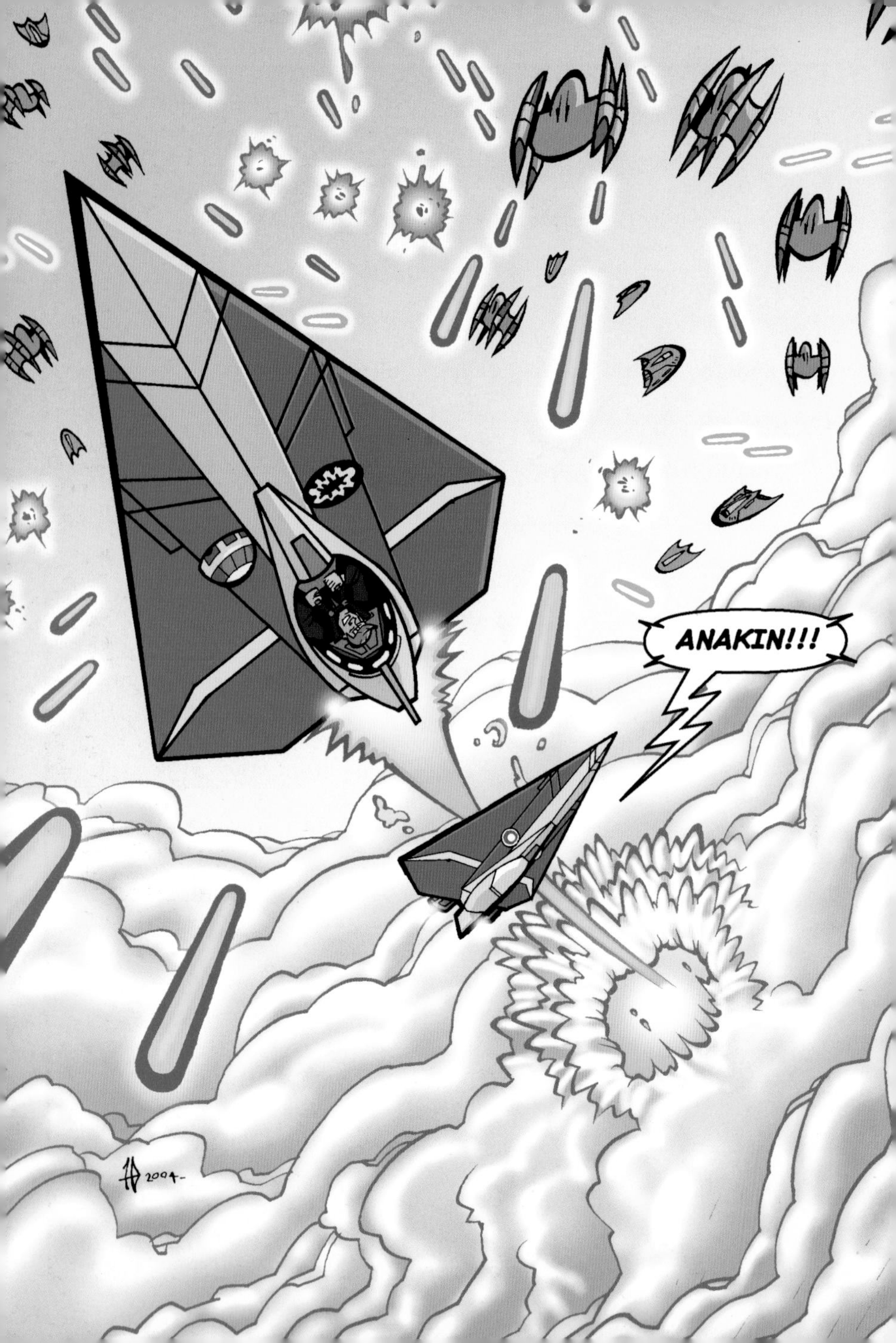
ANAKIN!!!

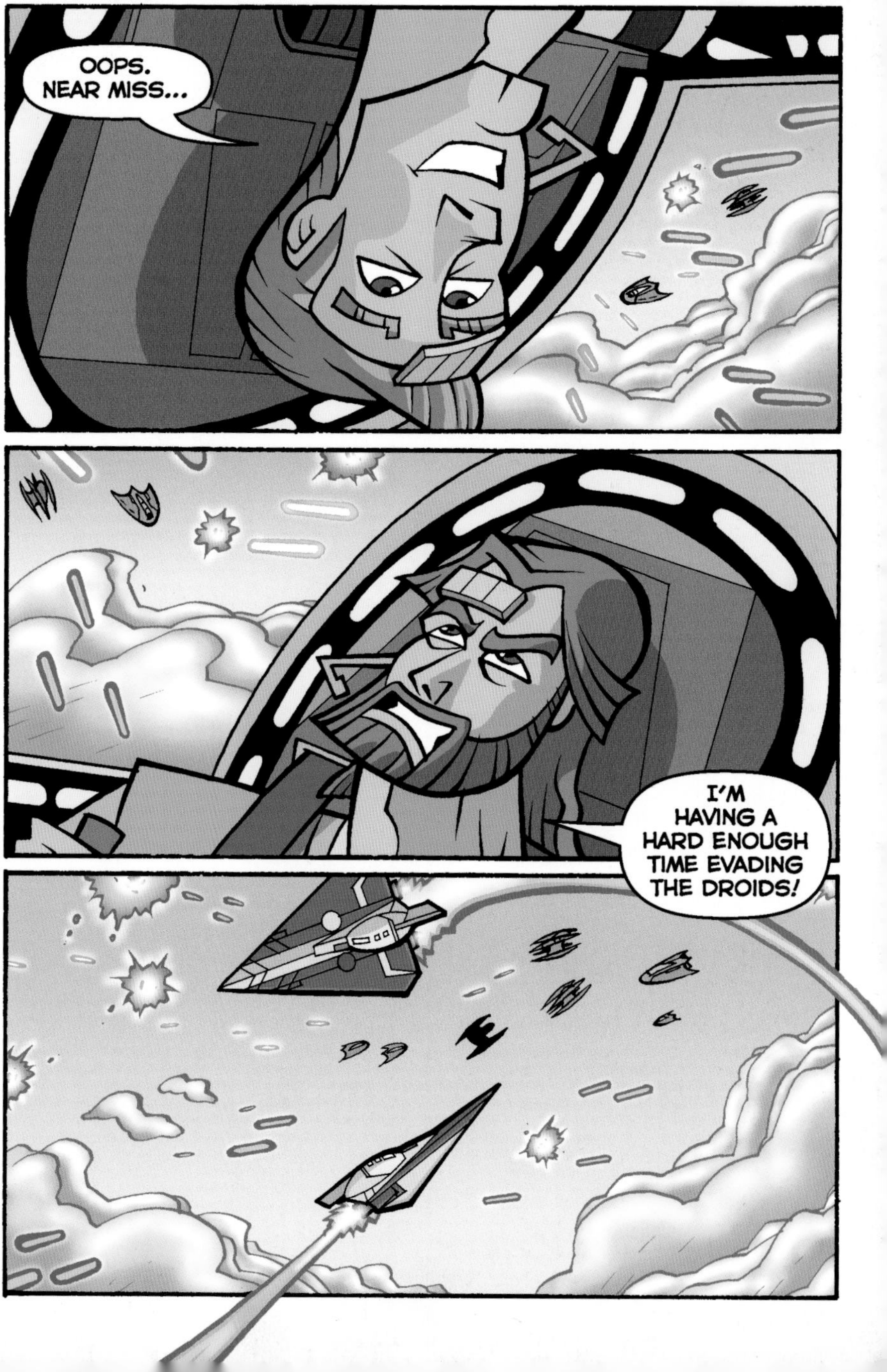
OOPS.
NEAR MISS...
I'M HAVING A HARD ENOUGH TIME EVADING THE DROIDS!

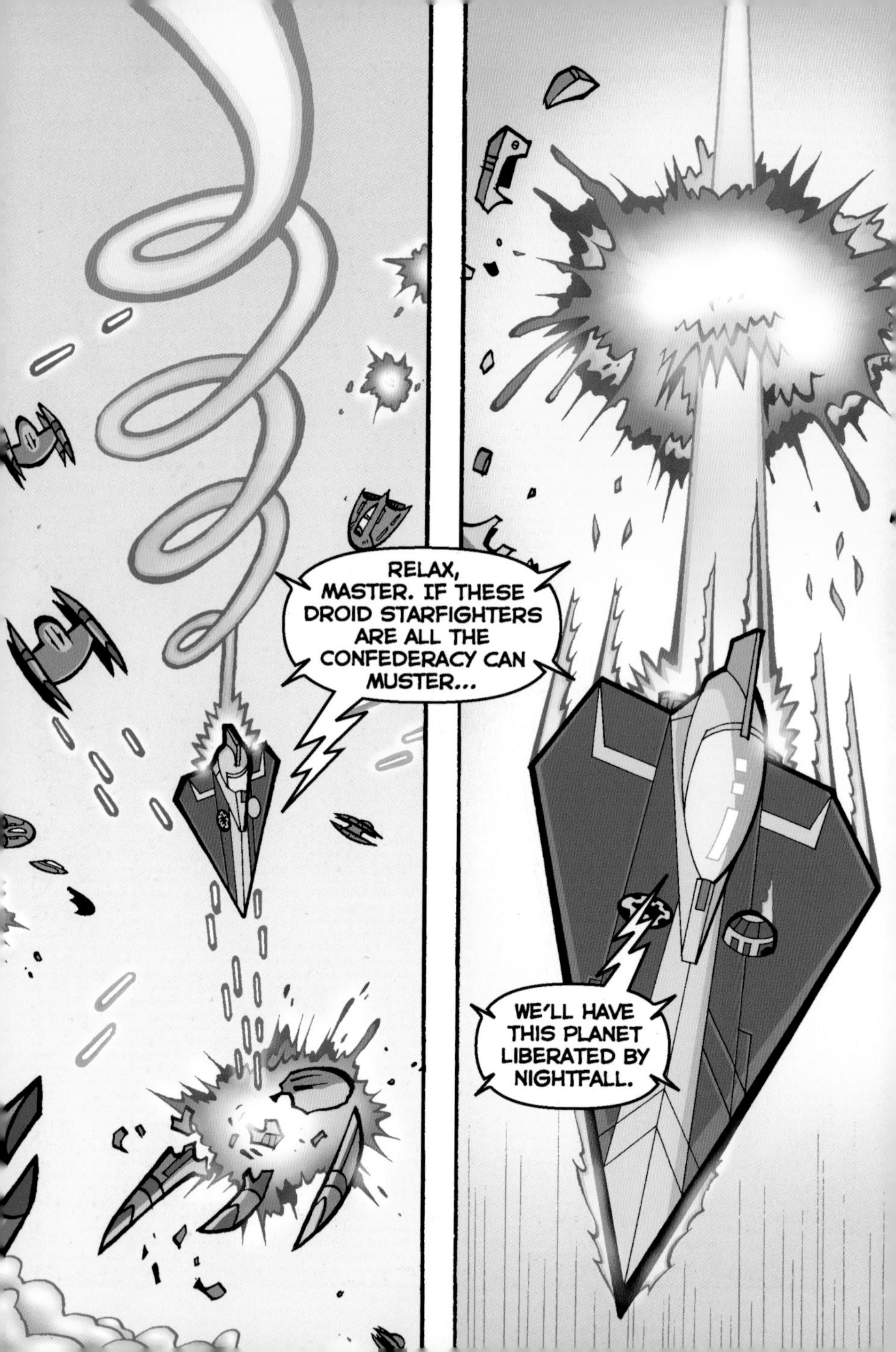
RELAX, MASTER. IF THESE DROID STARFIGHTERS ARE ALL THE CONFEDERACY CAN MUSTER...
WE'LL HAVE THIS PLANET LIBERATED BY NIGHTFALL.

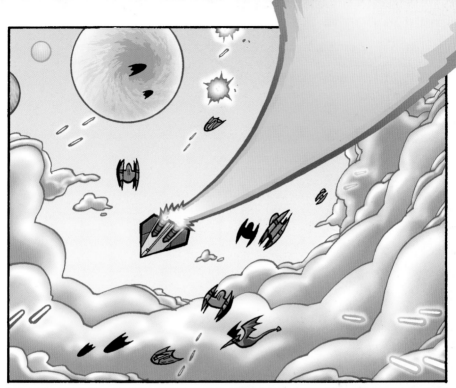

I'M GLAD YOU'RE SO CONFIDENT...

ESPECIALLY SINCE THIS PLANET'S ATMOSPHERE IS WREAKING HAVOC WITH MY SENSORS.

I'M FLYING BLI --

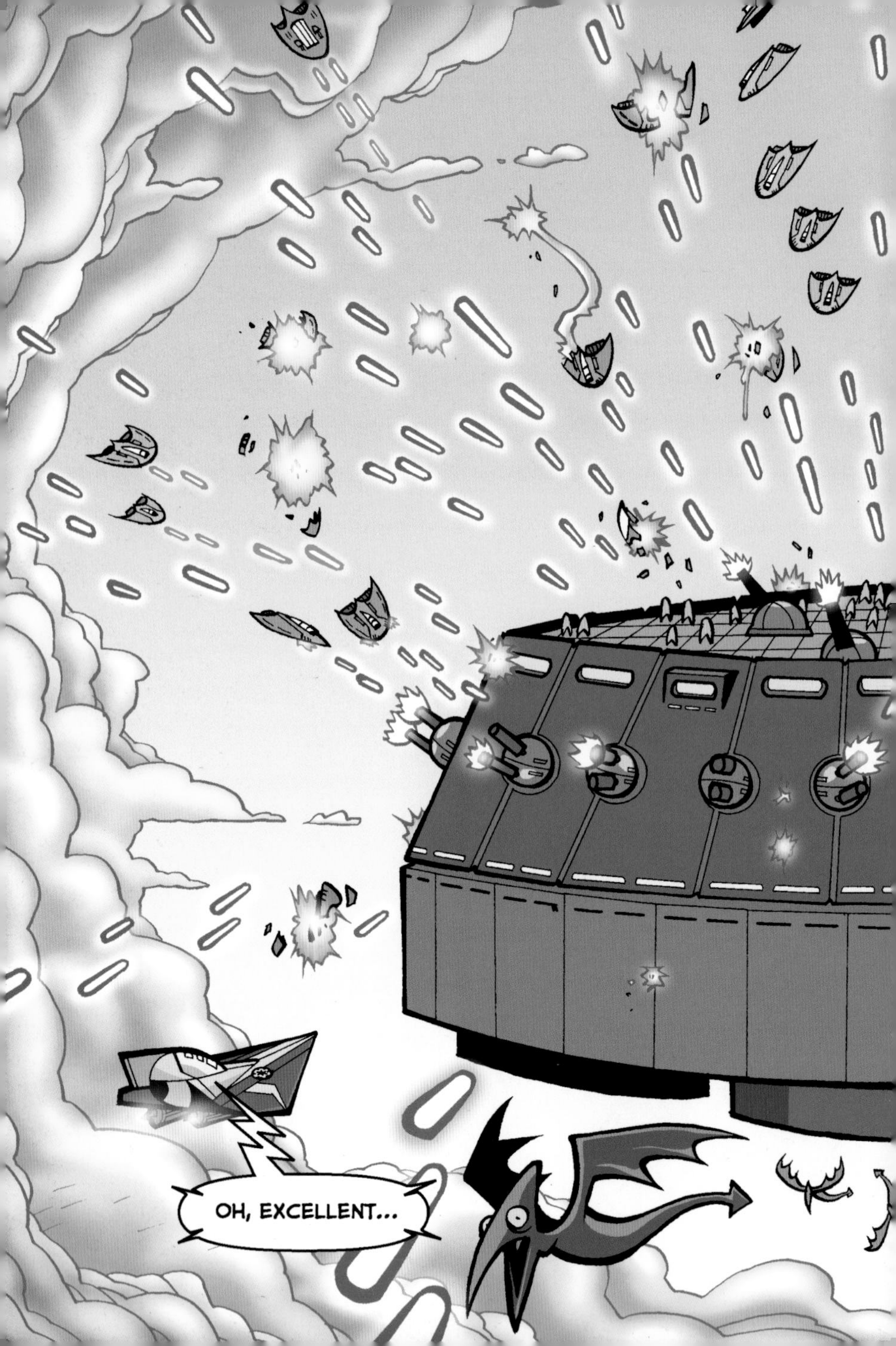
OH, EXCELLENT...

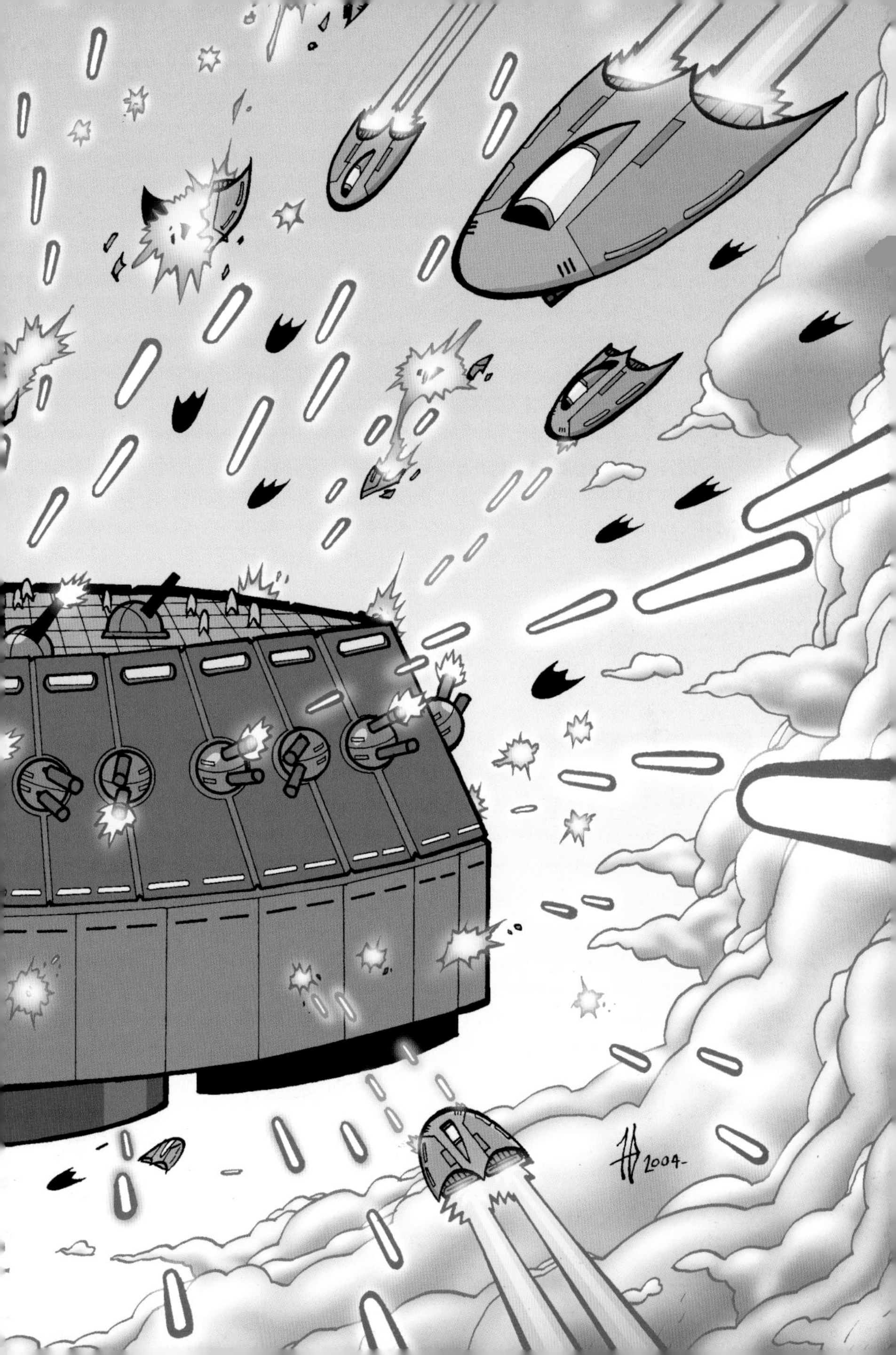
2004

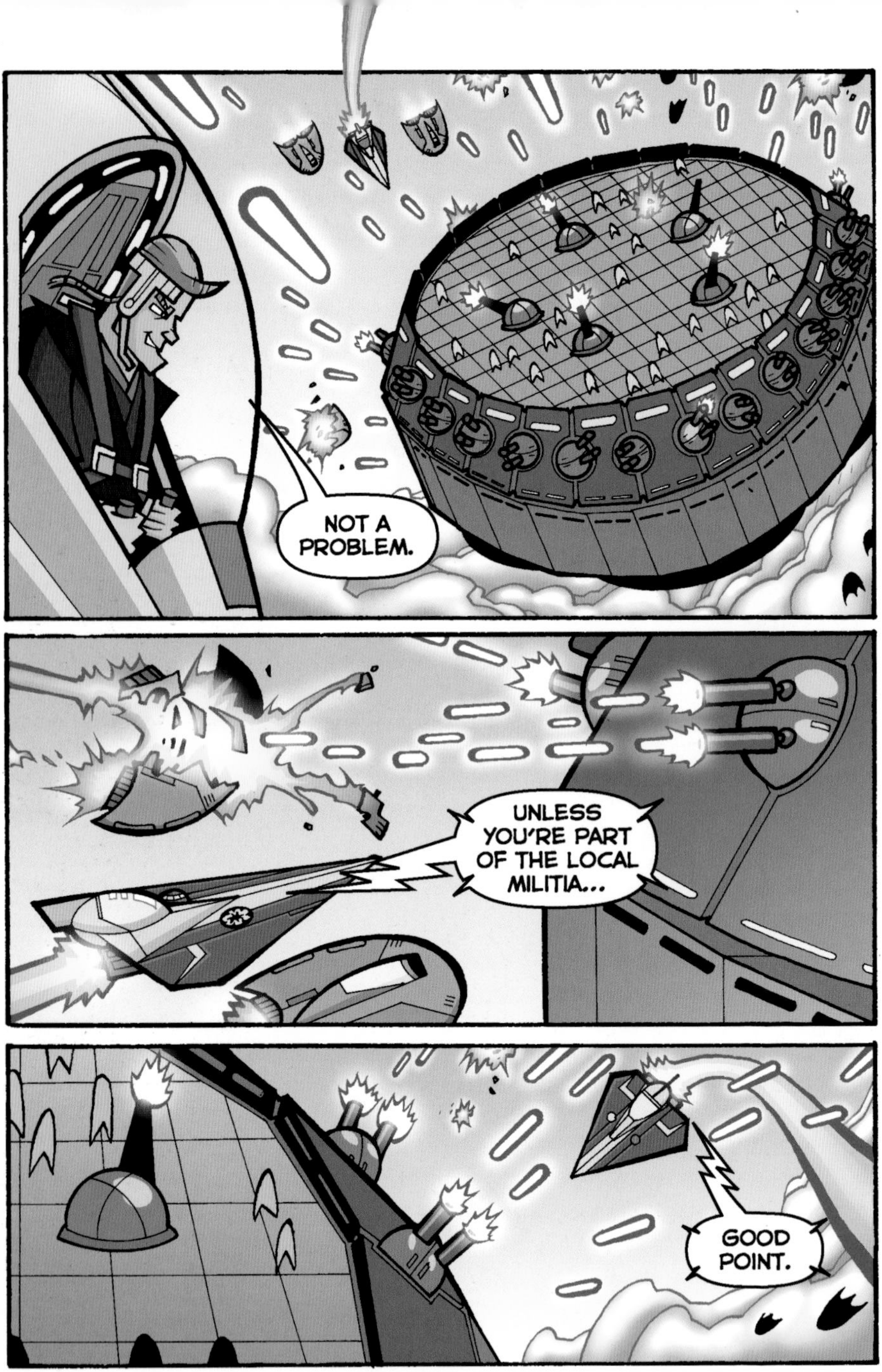
NOT A PROBLEM.
UNLESS YOU'RE PART OF THE LOCAL MILITIA...
GOOD POINT.

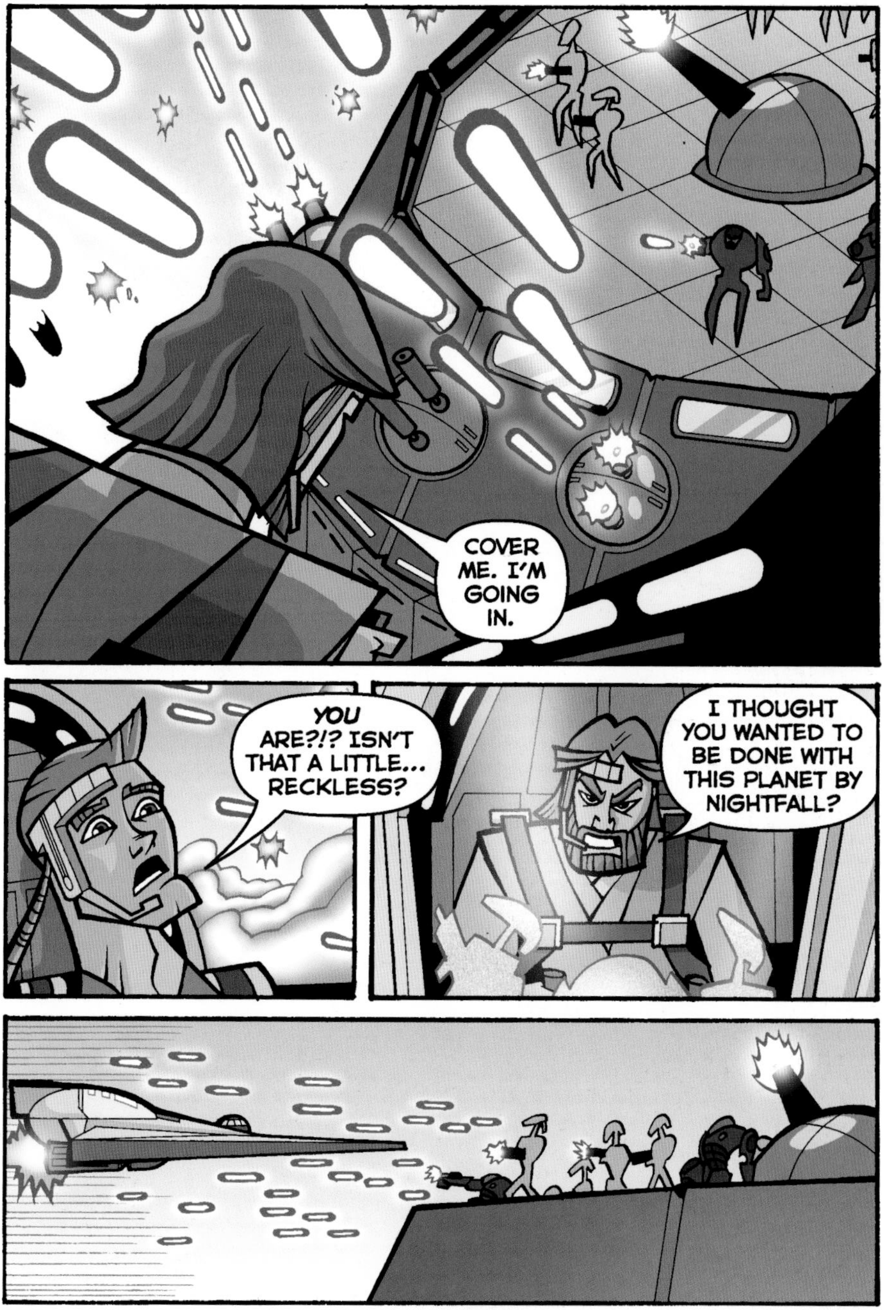
COVER ME. I'M GOING IN.
YOU ARE?!? ISN'T THAT A LITTLE... RECKLESS?
I THOUGHT YOU WANTED TO BE DONE WITH THIS PLANET BY NIGHTFALL?

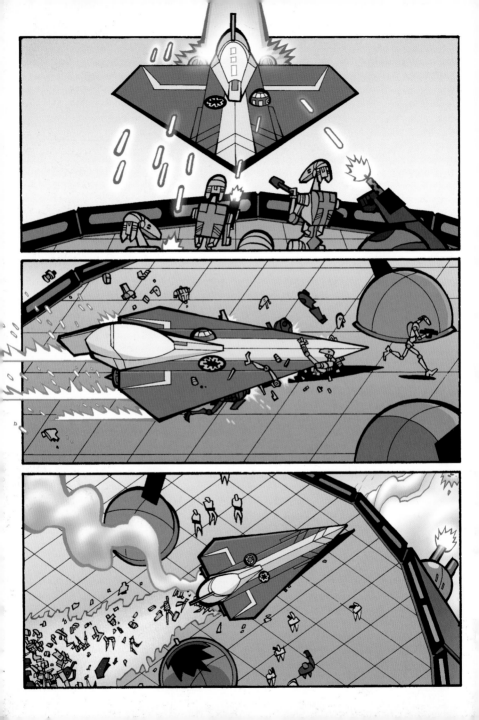

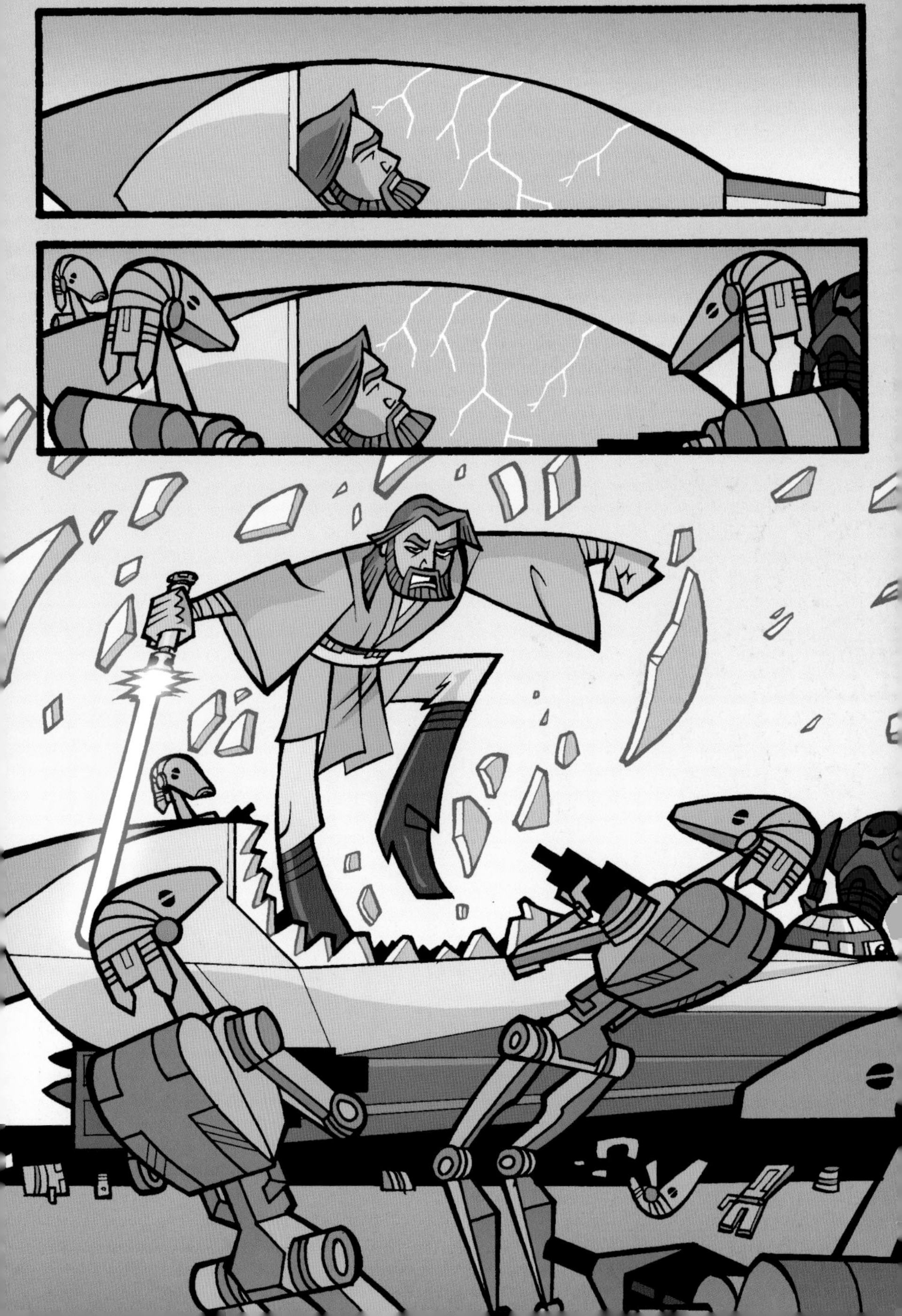

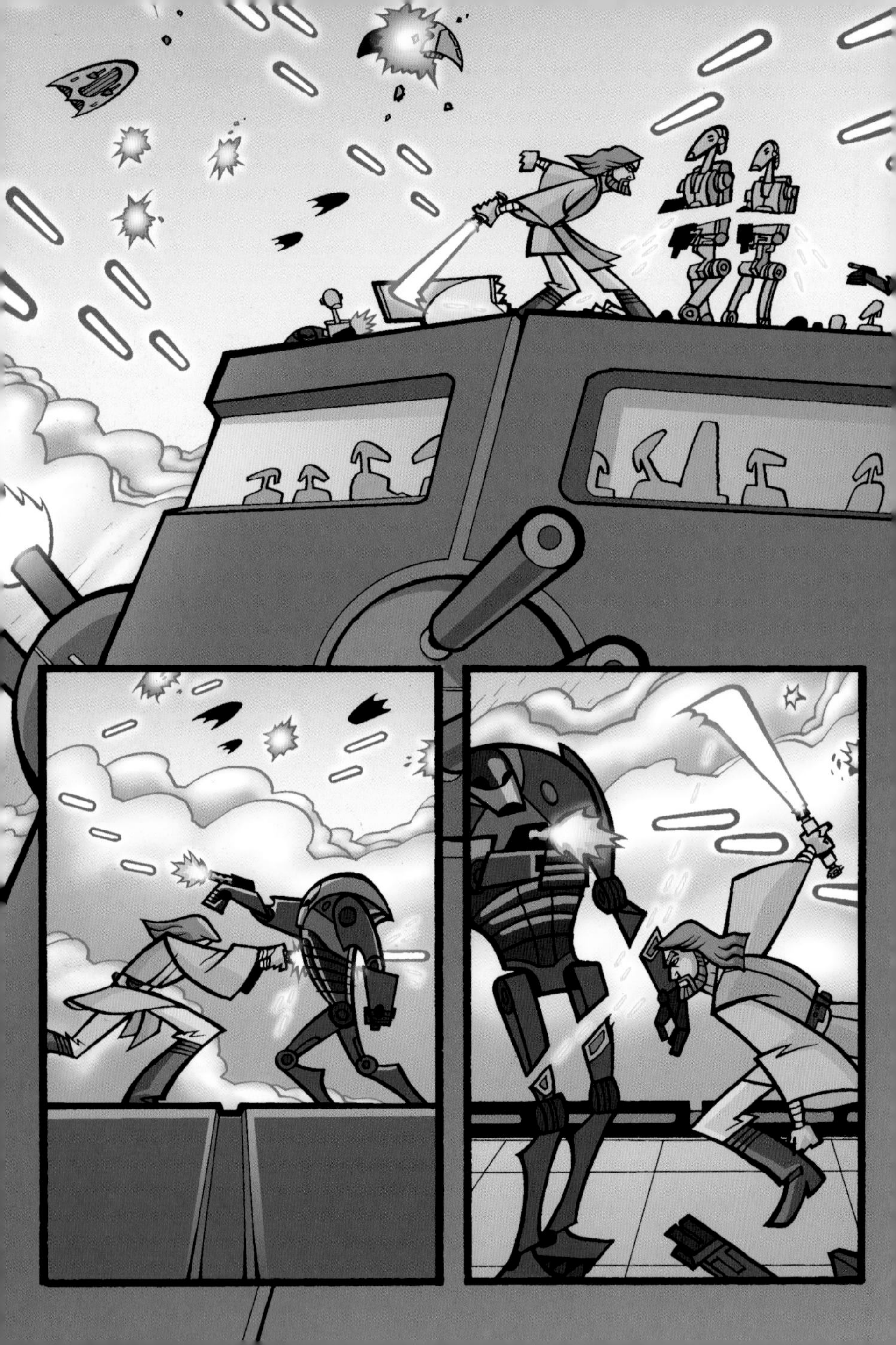

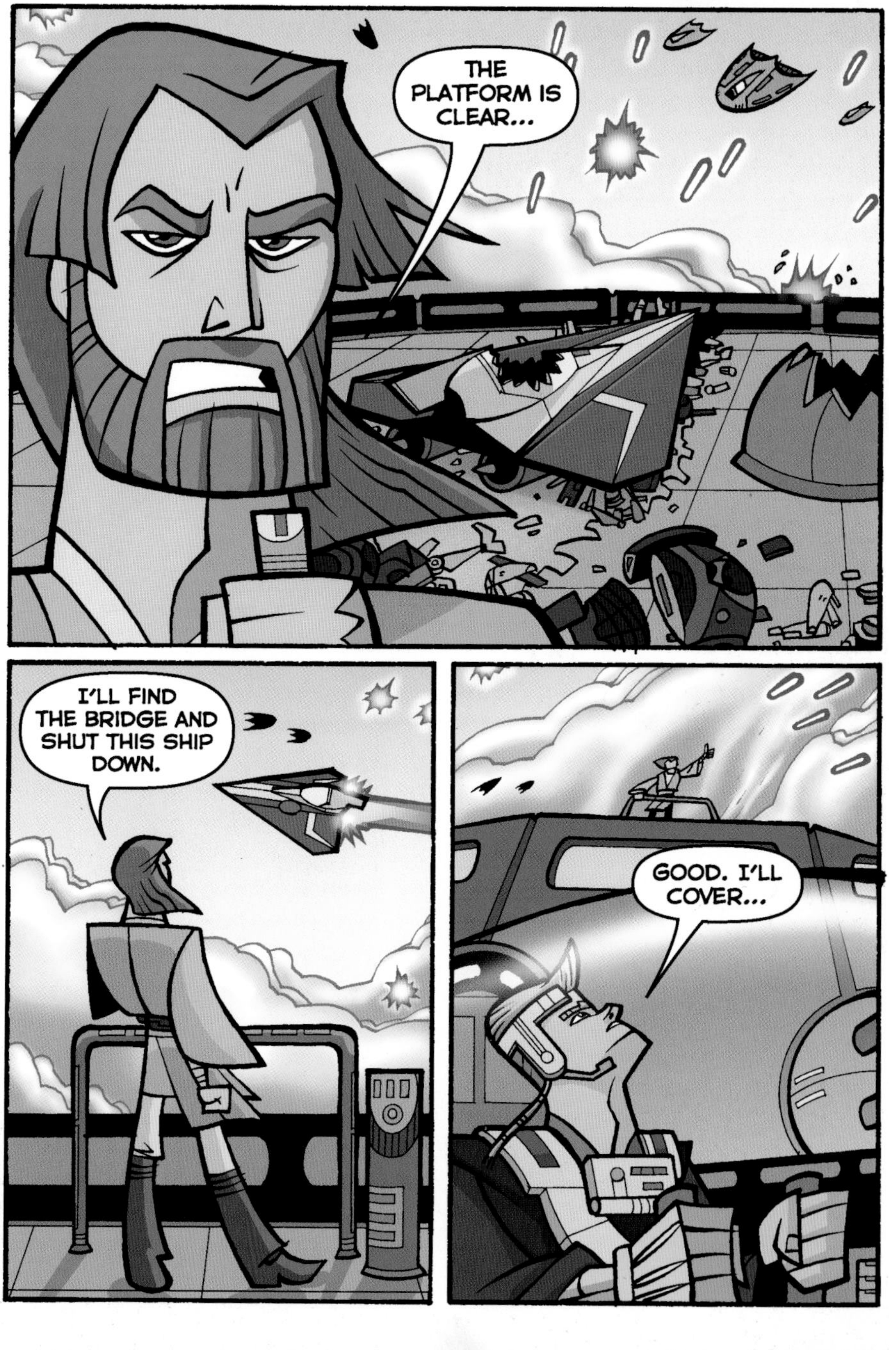
THE PLATFORM IS CLEAR...
I'LL FIND THE BRIDGE AND SHUT THIS SHIP DOWN.
GOOD. I'LL COVER...

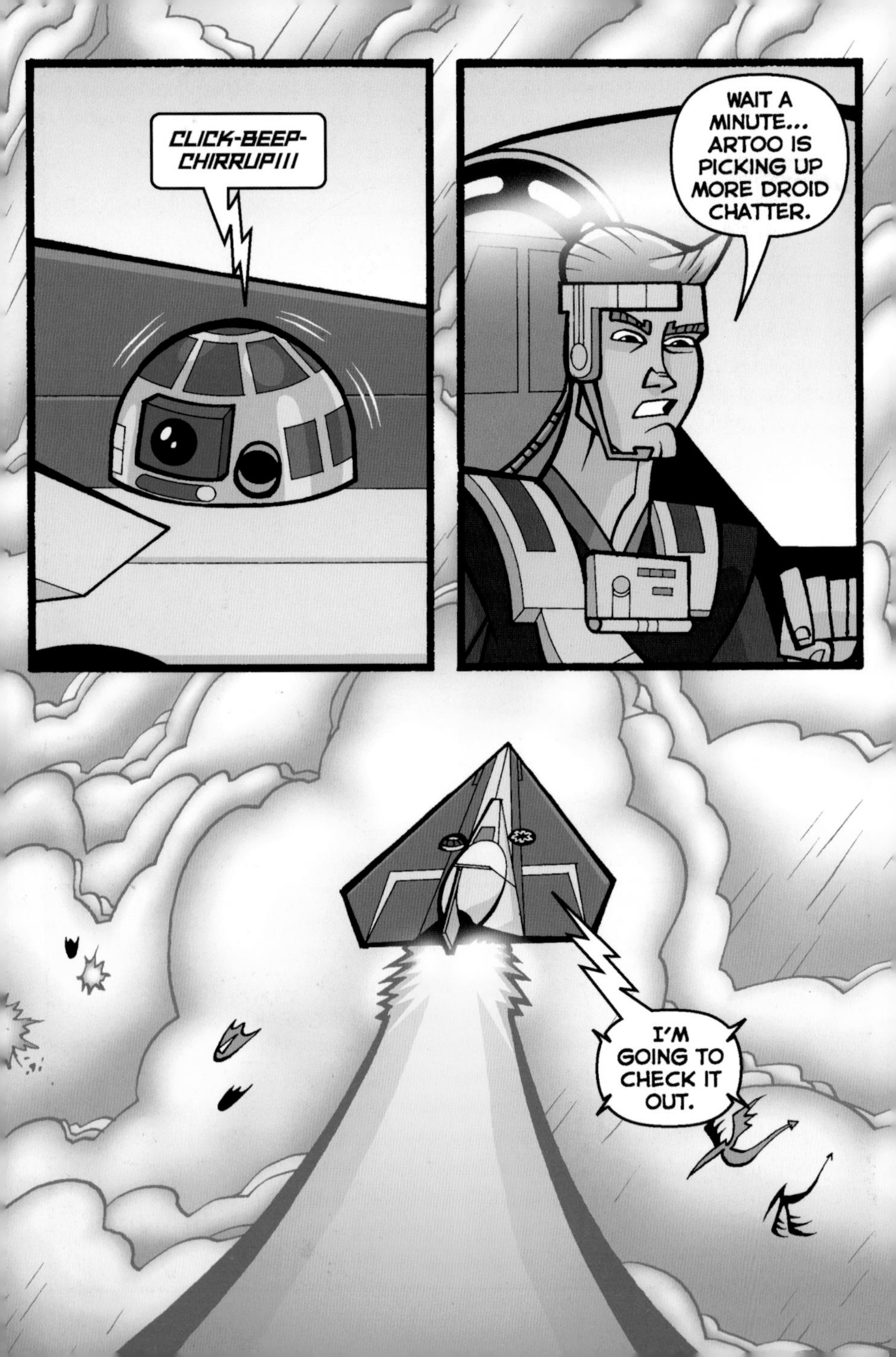
CLICK-BEEP-CHIRRUP!!!
WAIT A MINUTE... ARTOO IS PICKING UP MORE DROID CHATTER.
I'M GOING TO CHECK IT OUT.

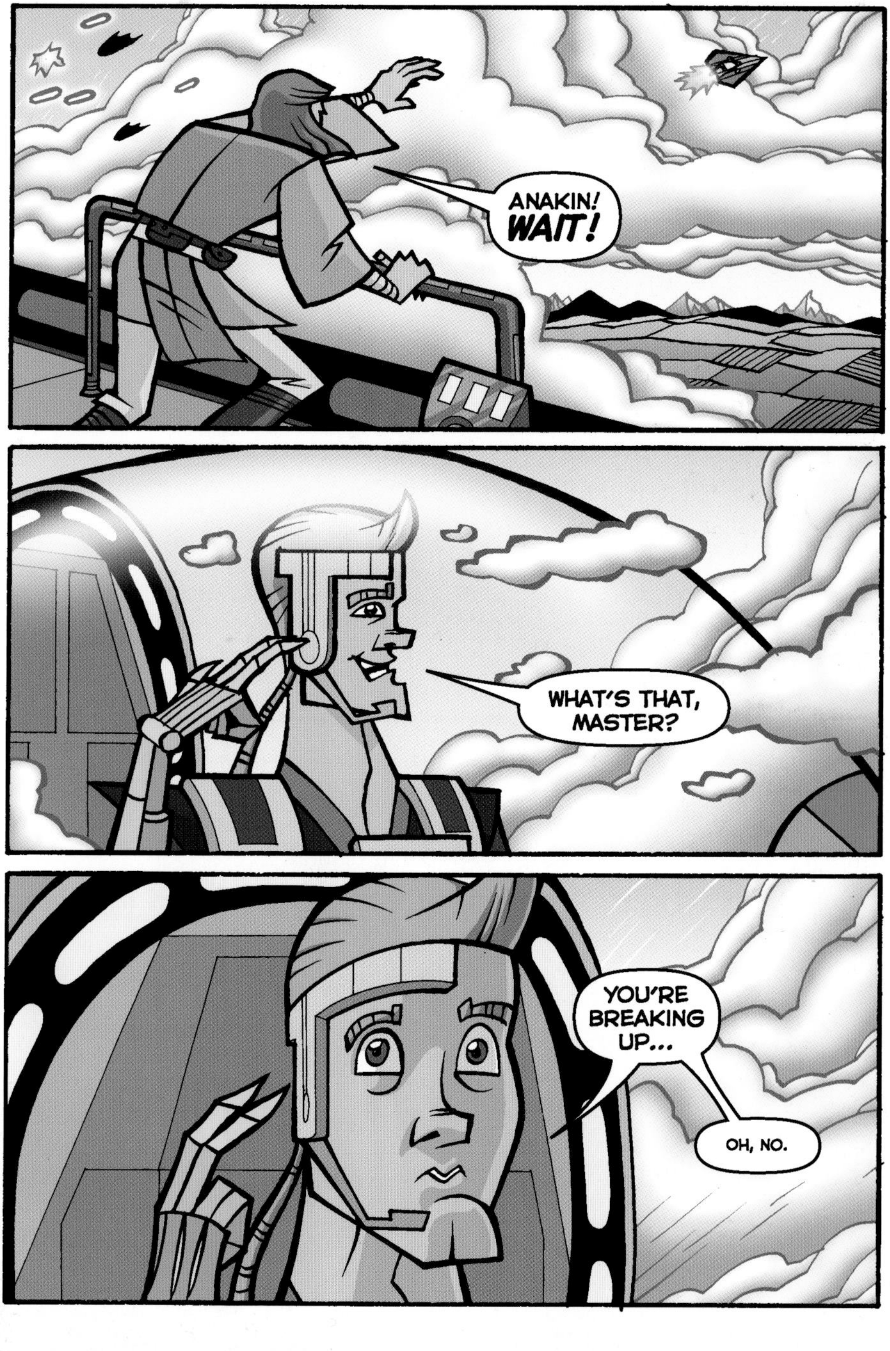
ANAKIN! WAIT!
WHAT'S THAT, MASTER?
YOU'RE BREAKING UP...
OH, NO.

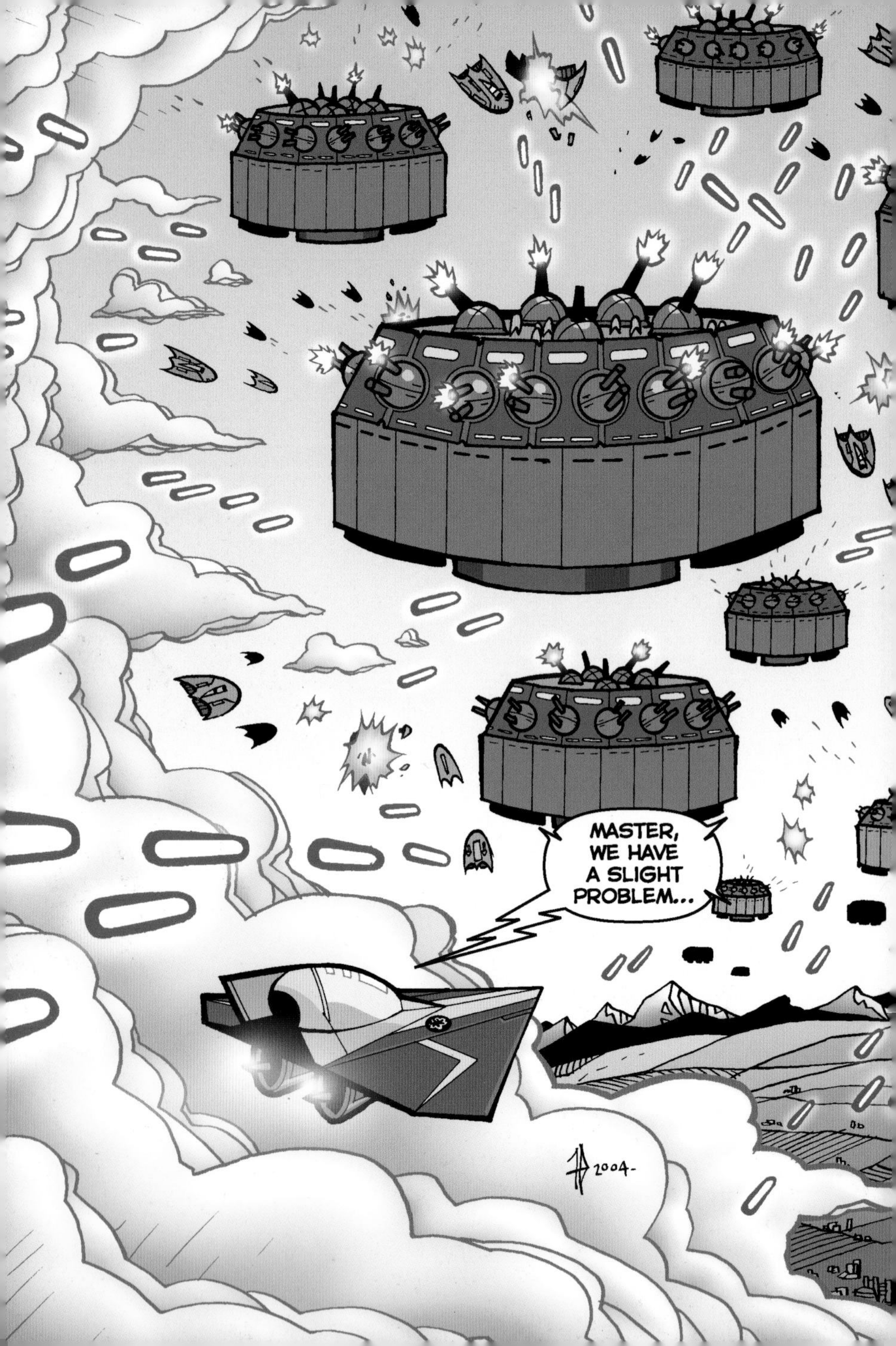
MASTER, WE HAVE A SLIGHT PROBLEM...
2004

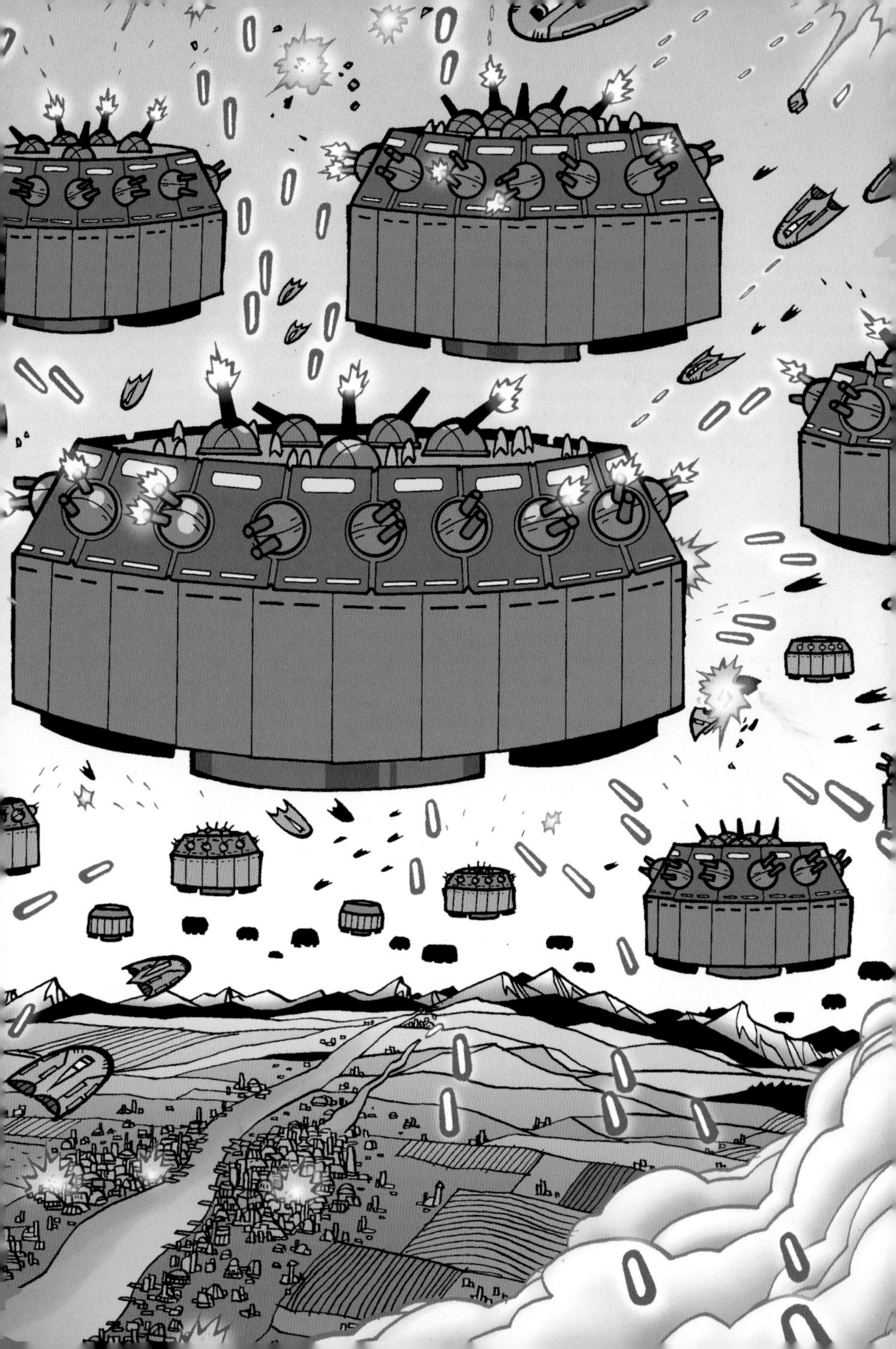

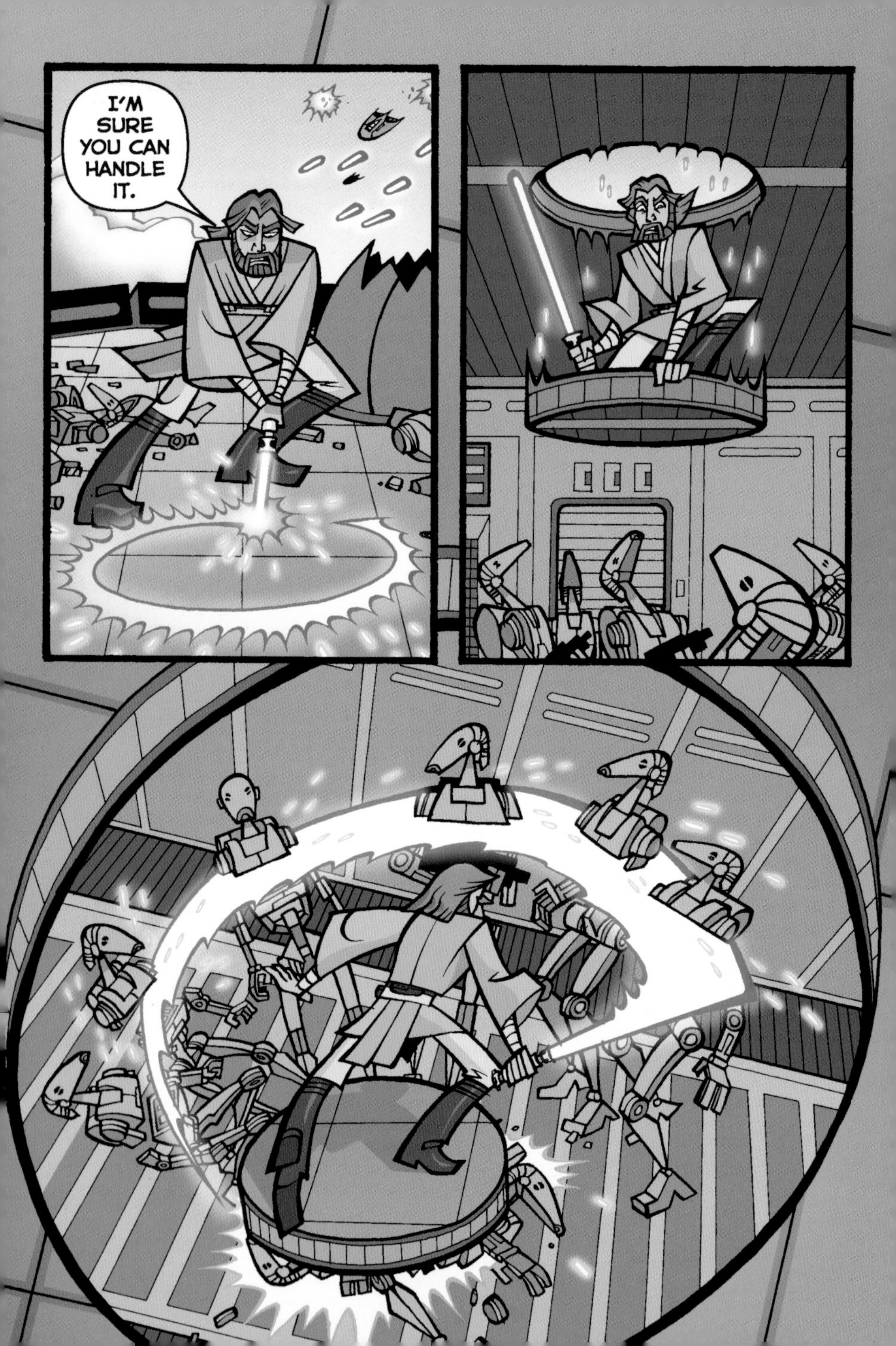
I'M SURE YOU CAN HANDLE IT.

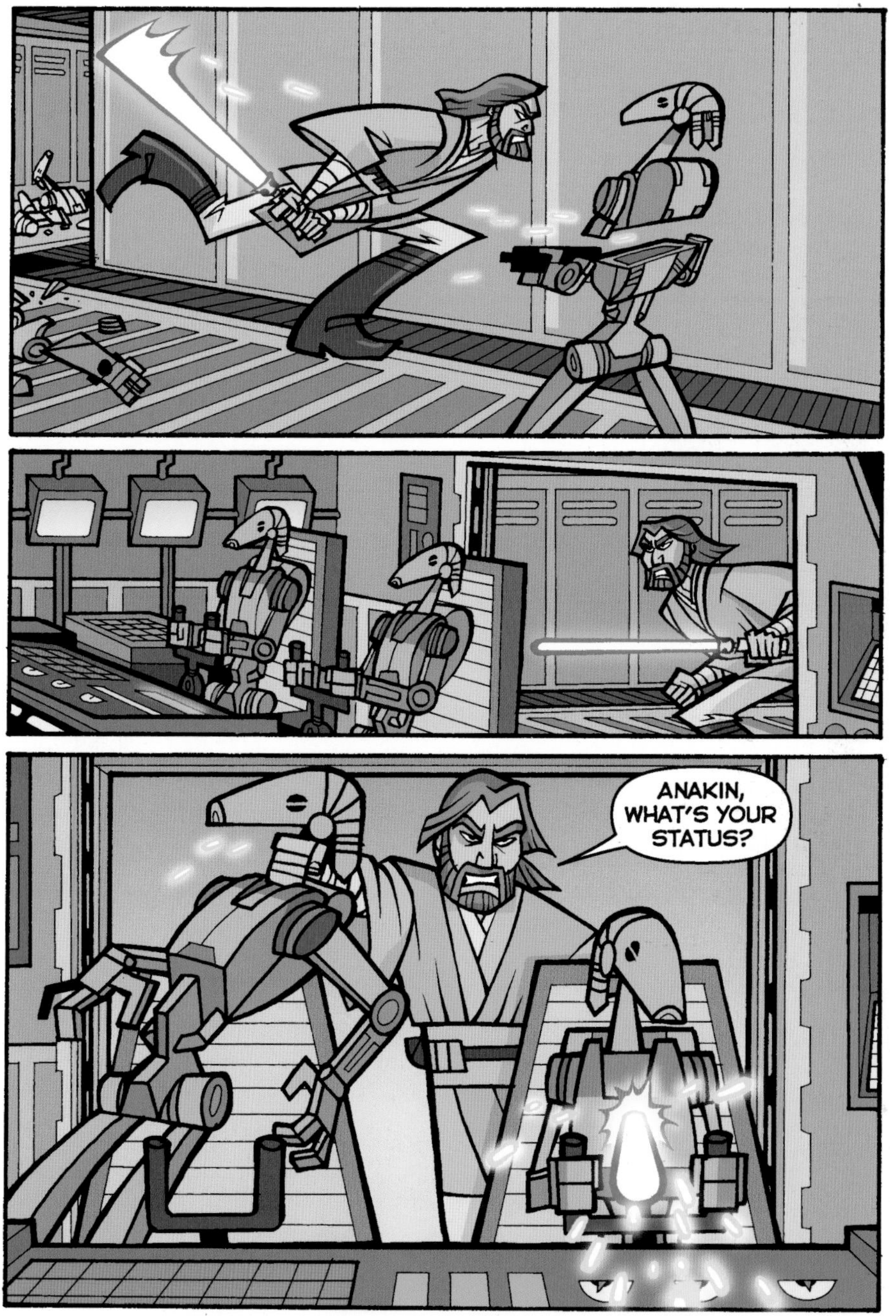
ANAKIN, WHAT'S YOUR STATUS?

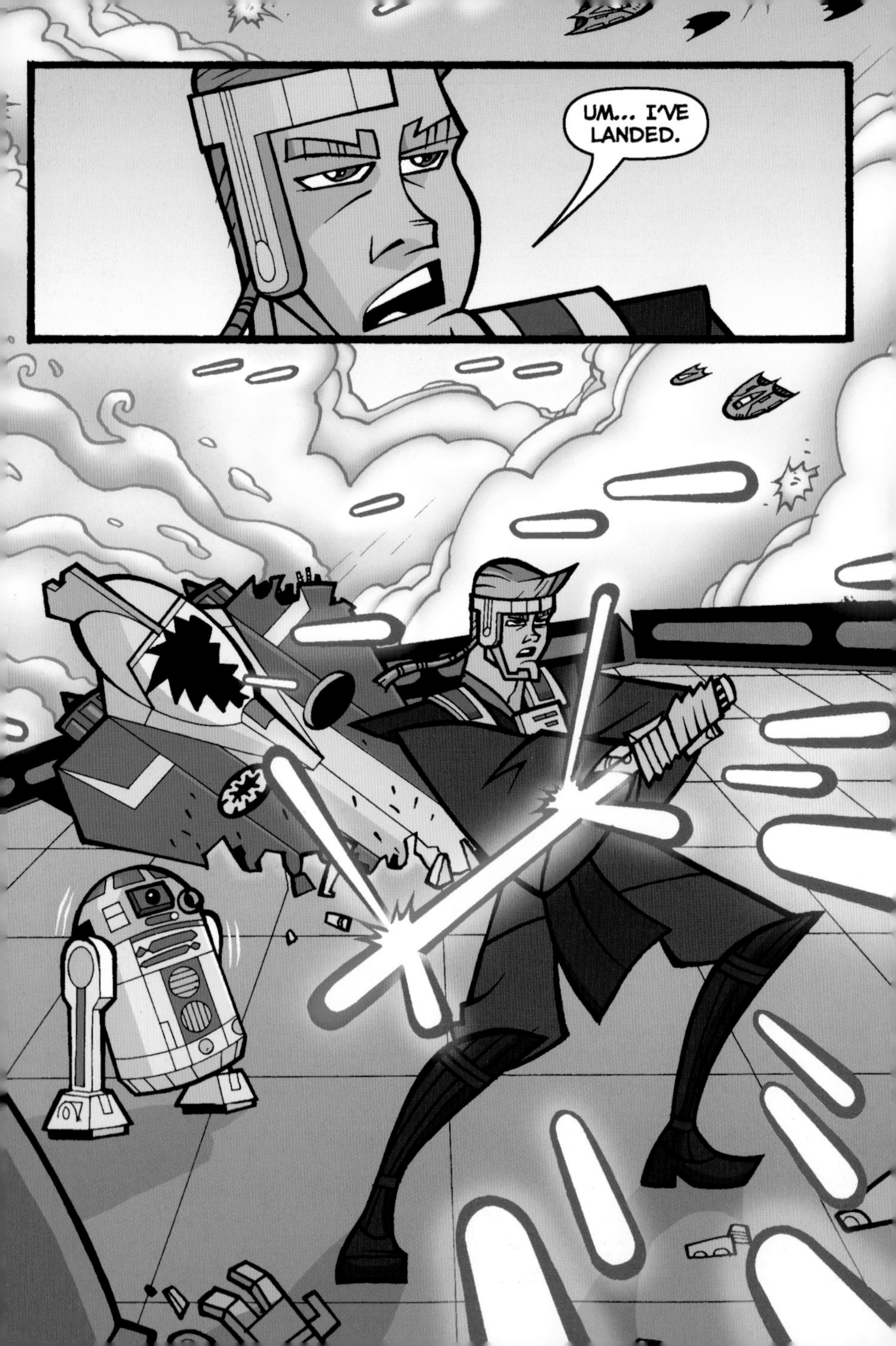
UM... I'VE LANDED.

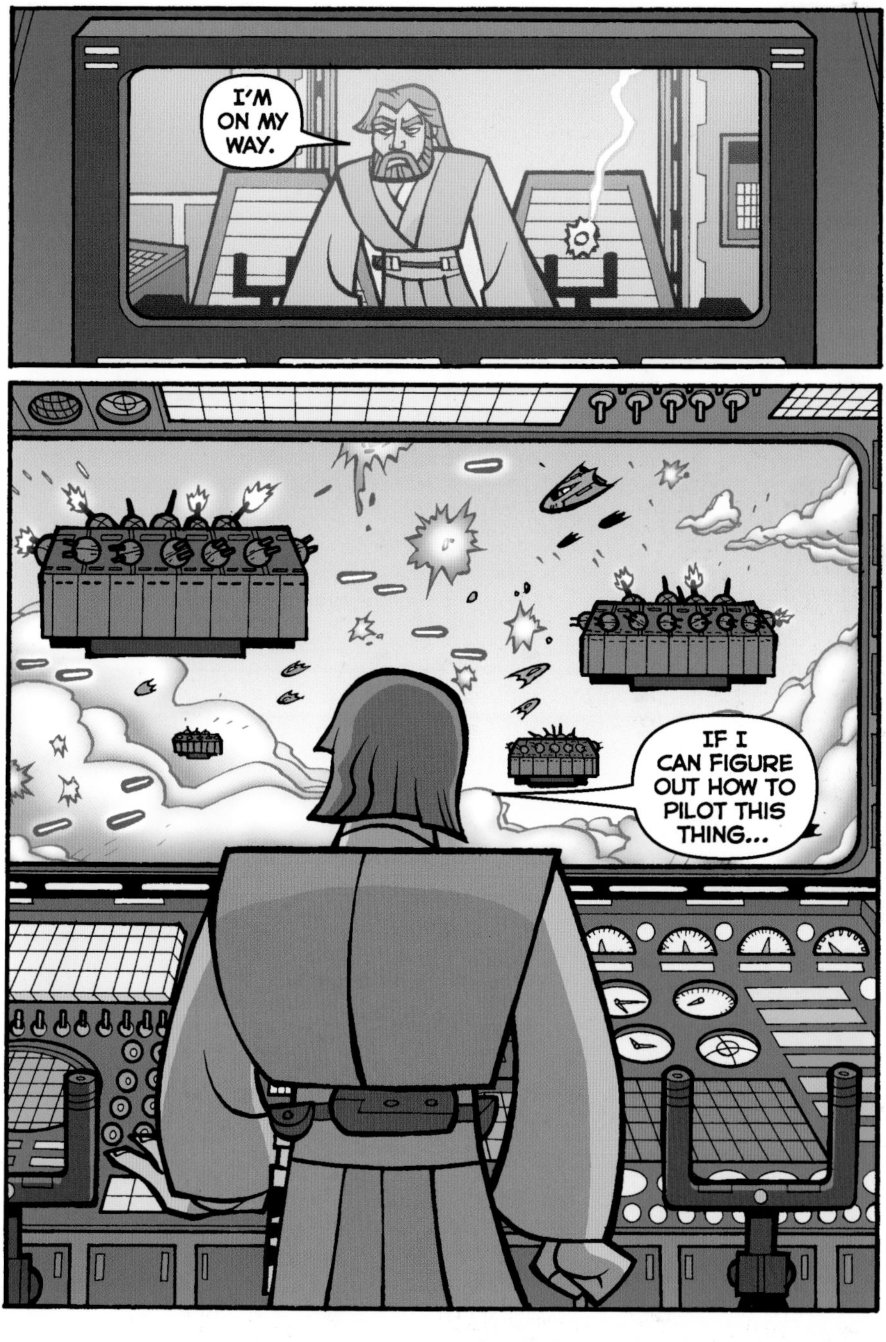
I'M ON MY WAY.
IF I CAN FIGURE OUT HOW TO PILOT THIS THING...

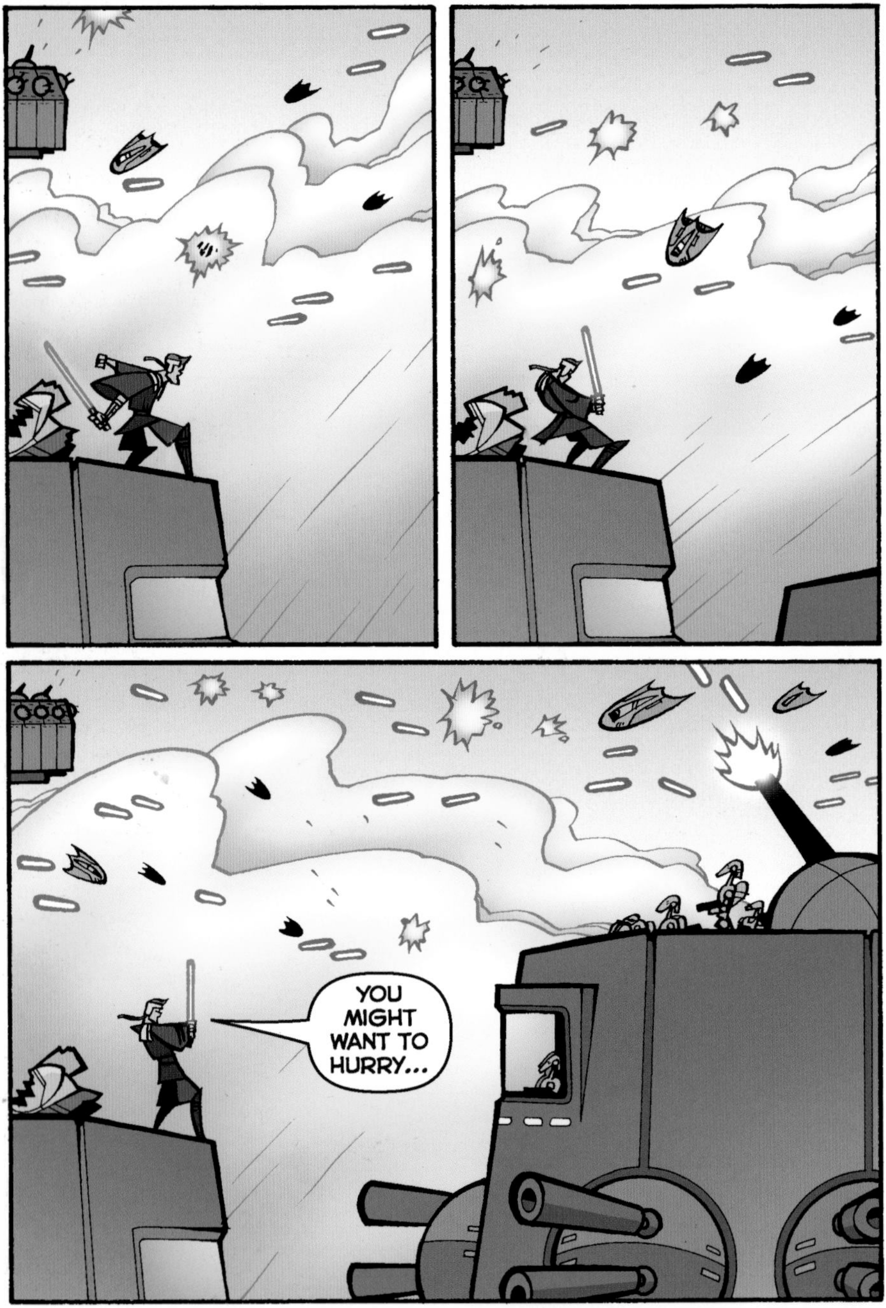
YOU MIGHT WANT TO HURRY...

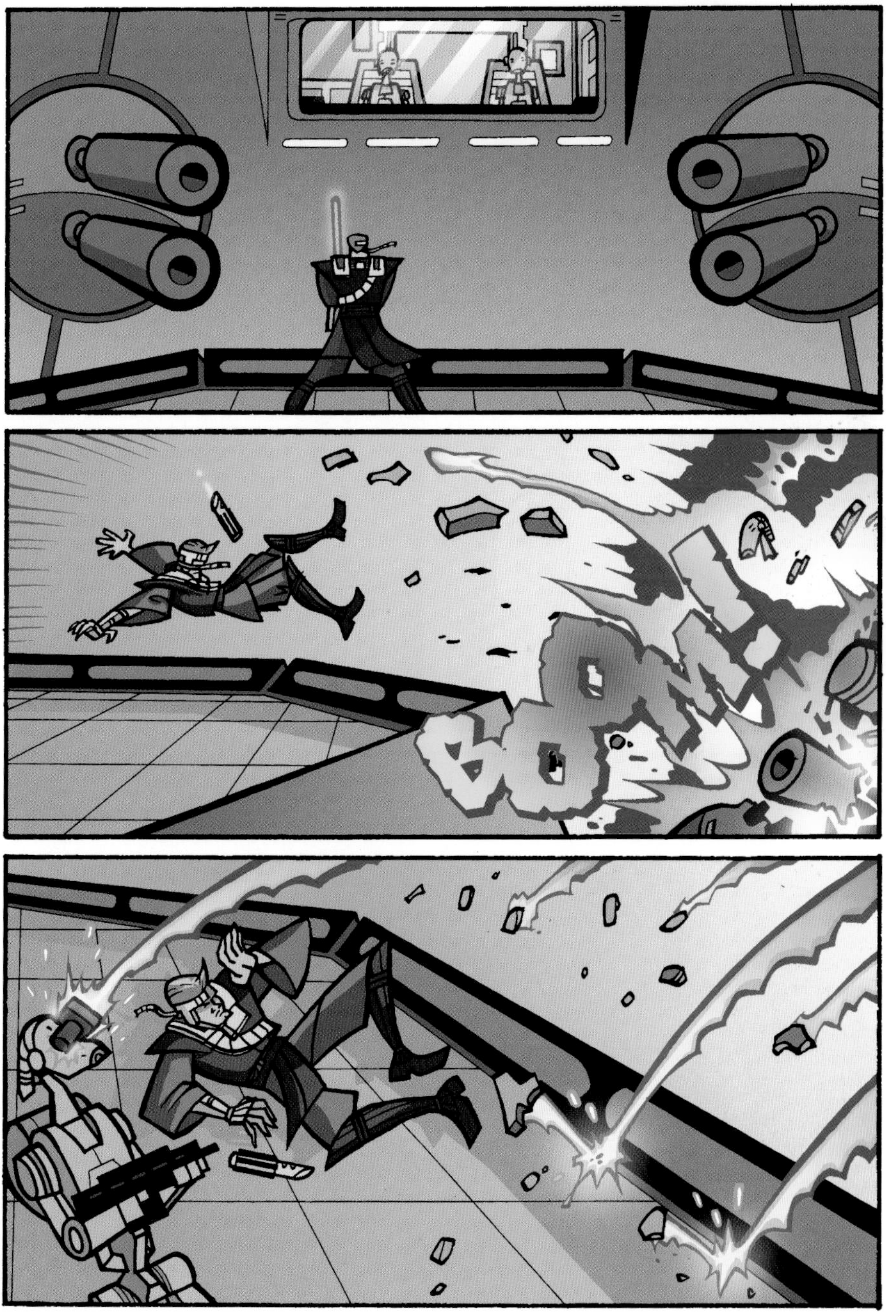
BOOM

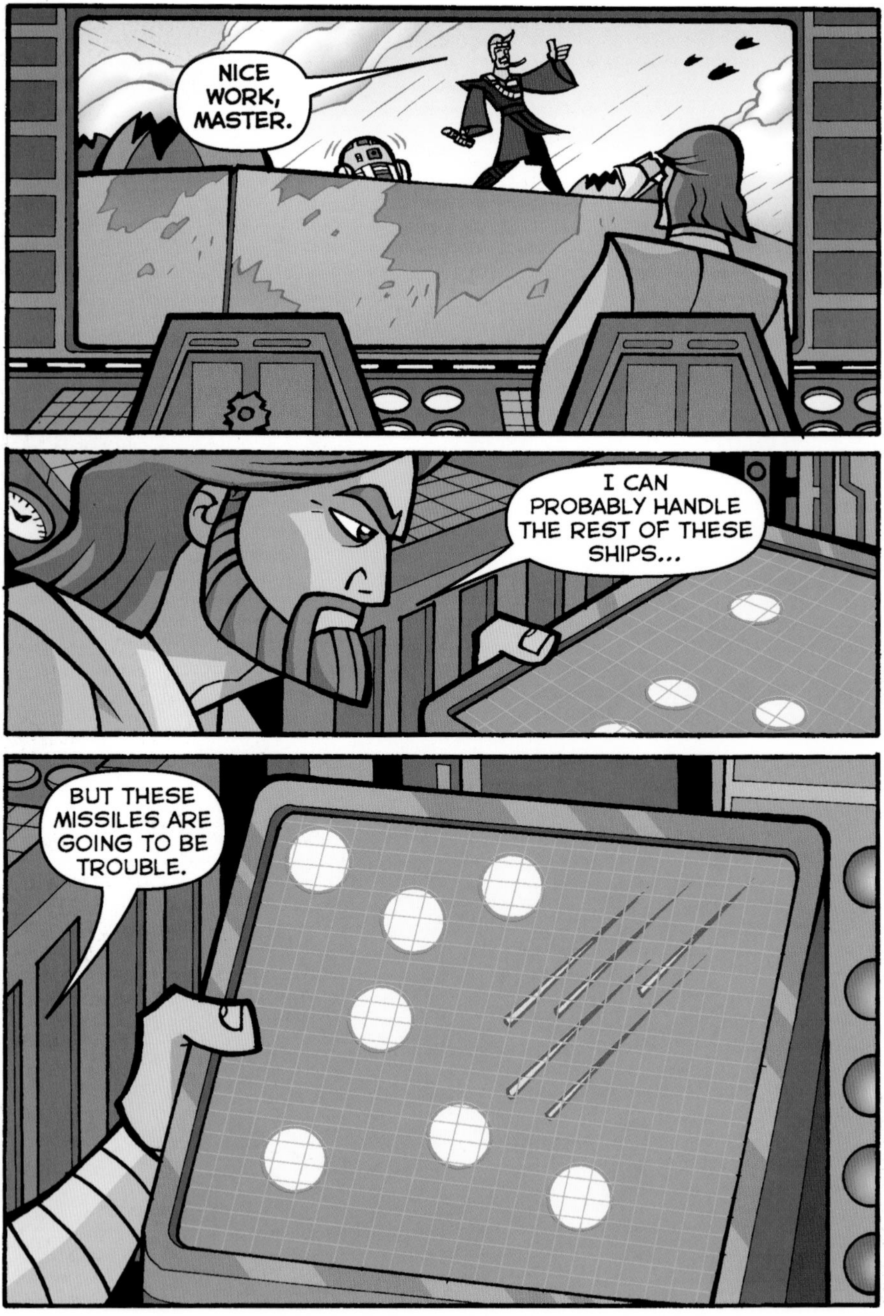
NICE WORK, MASTER.
I CAN PROBABLY HANDLE THE REST OF THESE SHIPS...
BUT THESE MISSILES ARE GOING TO BE TROUBLE.

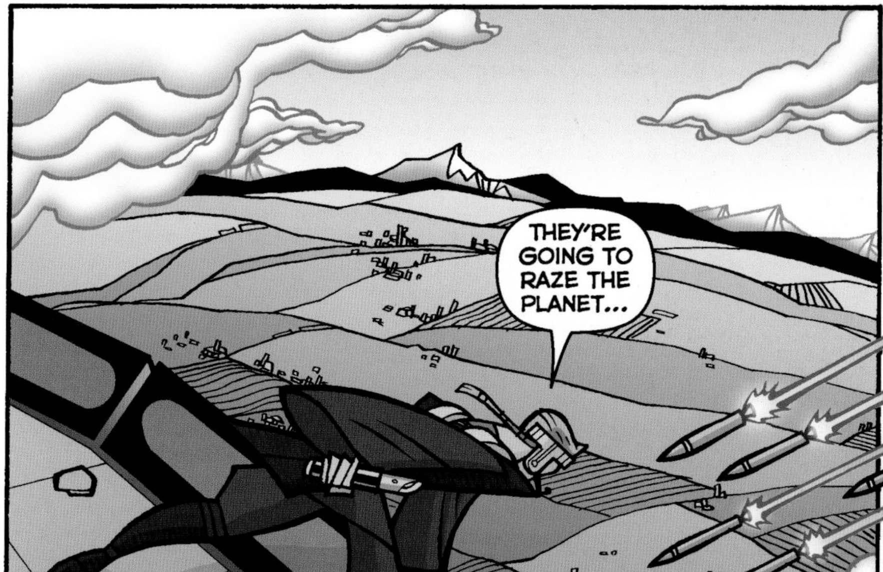
THEY'RE GOING TO RAZE THE PLANET...

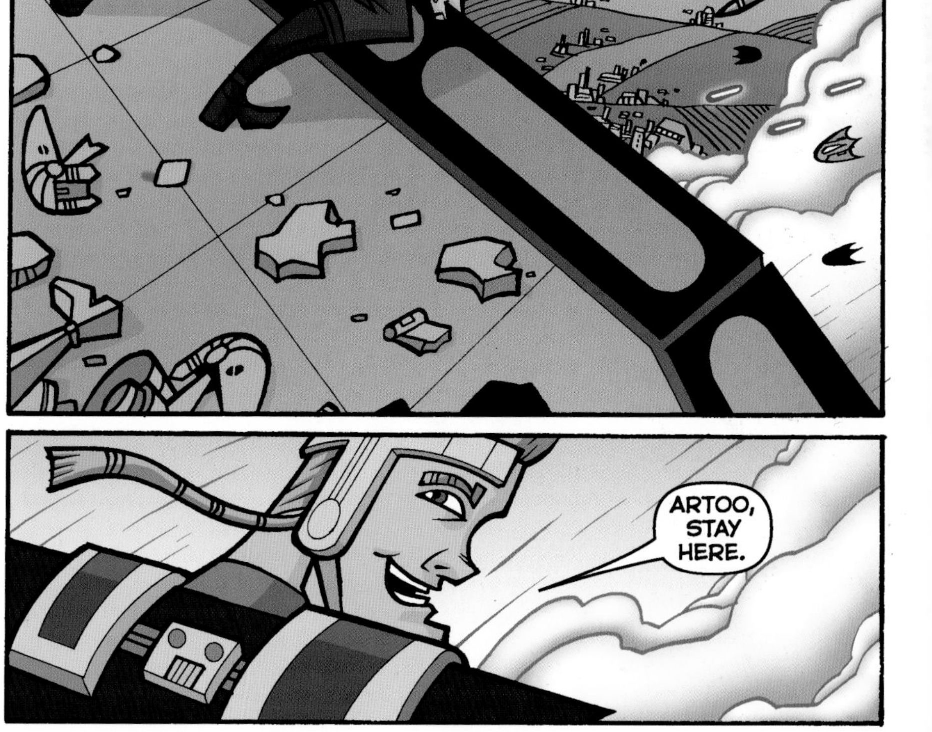
ARTOO, STAY HERE.

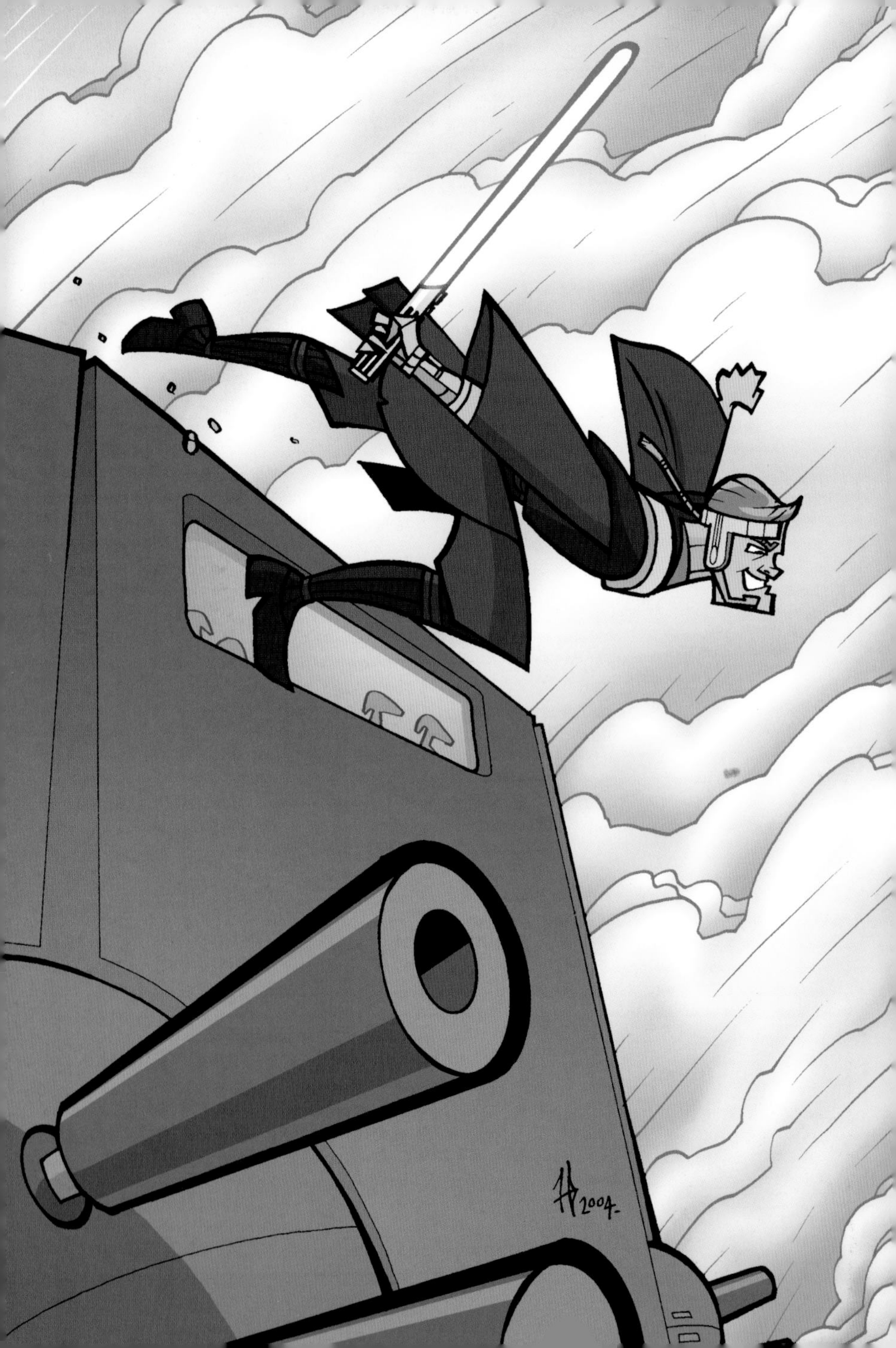
2004

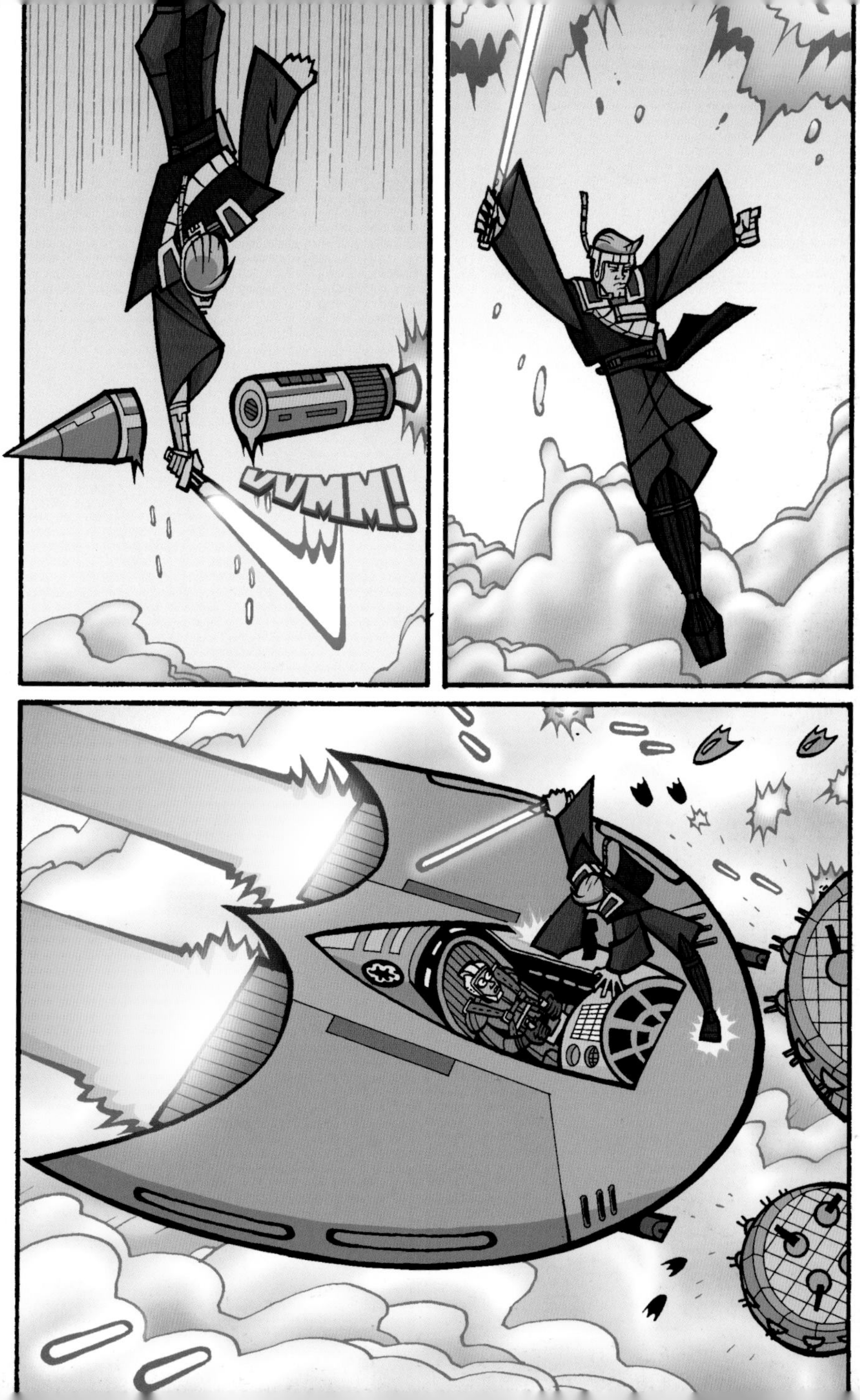
VVMM!

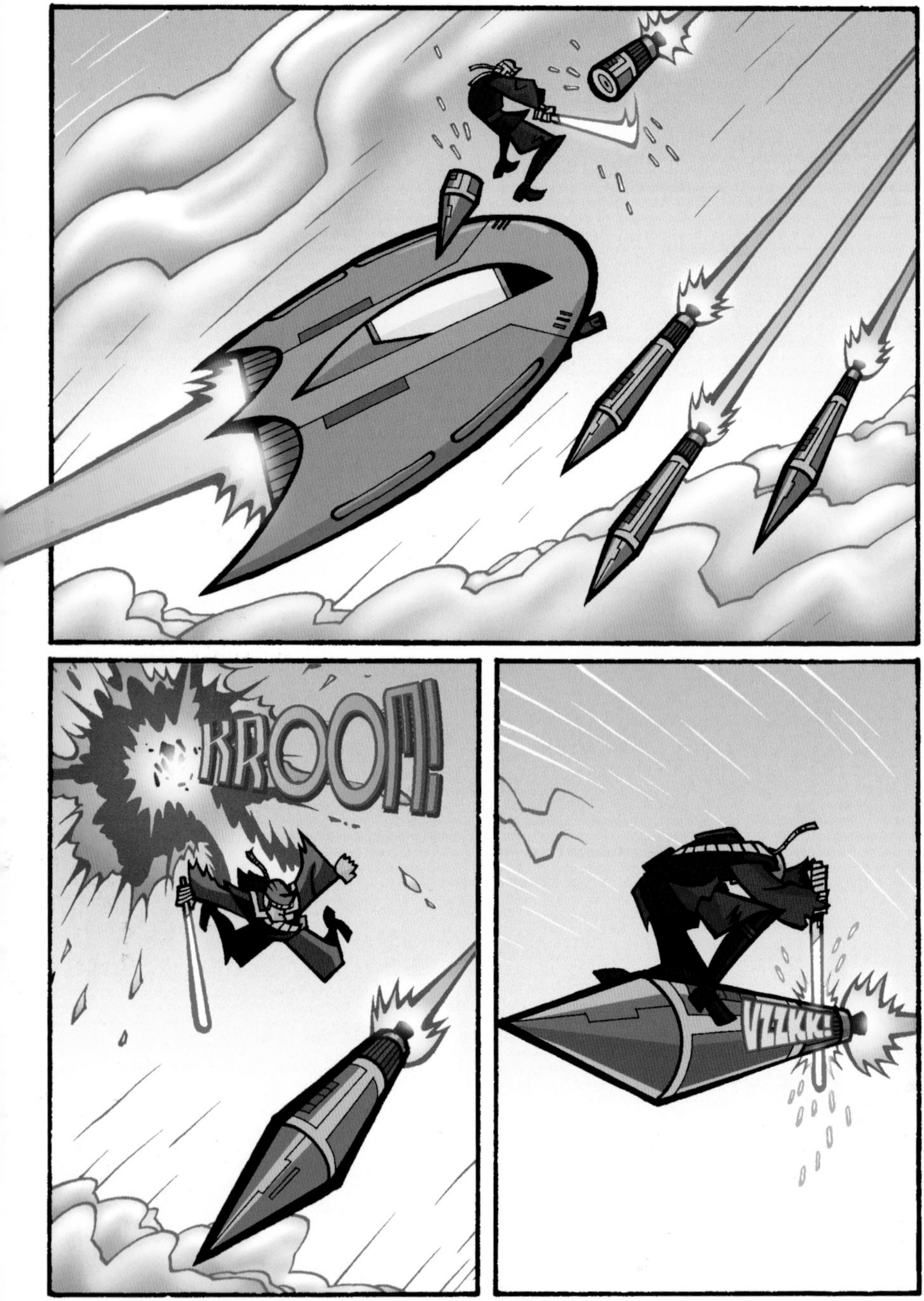
KROOM!
VZZKK!

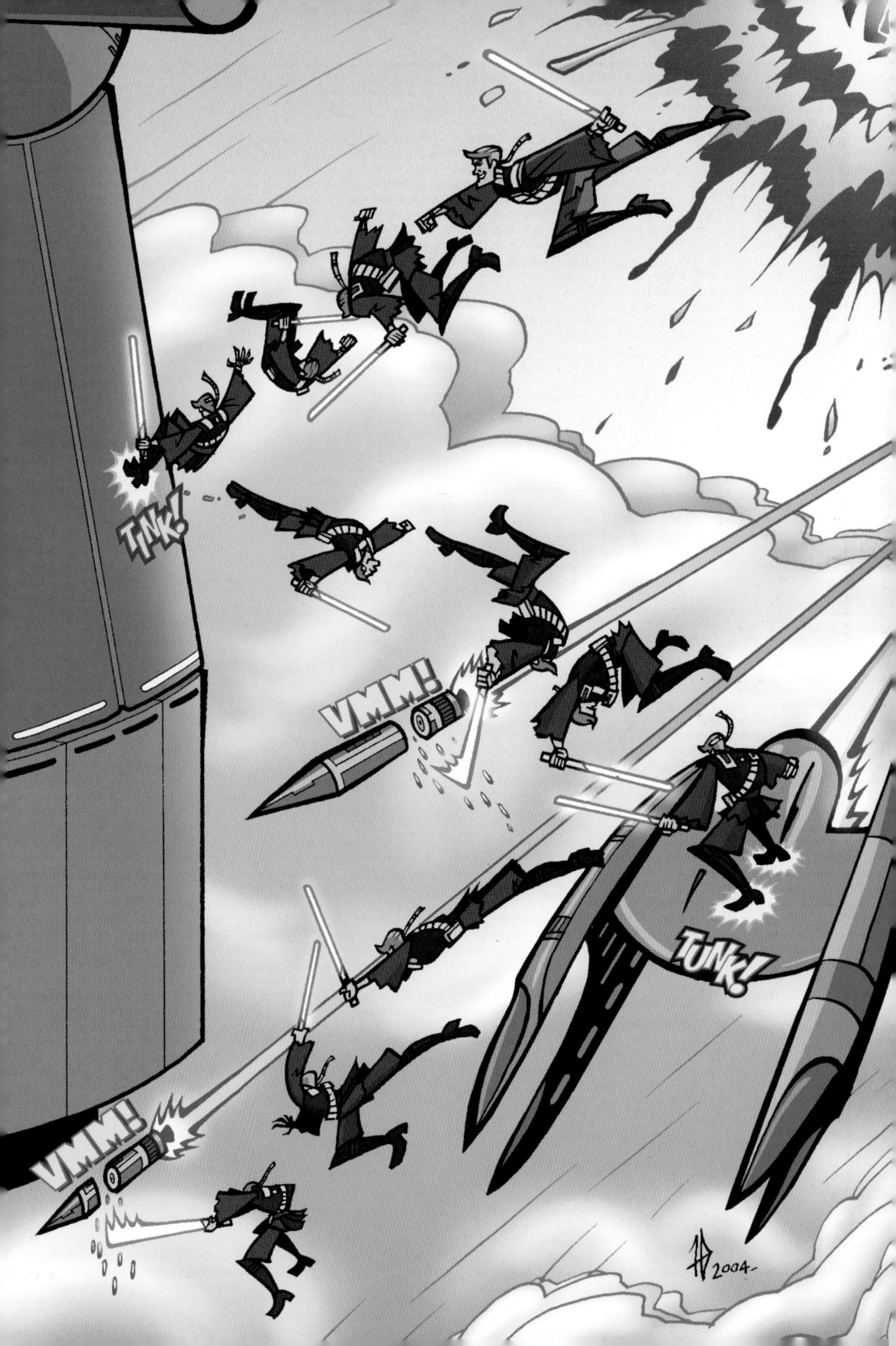
TINK!
VMM!
TUNK!
VMM!
2004

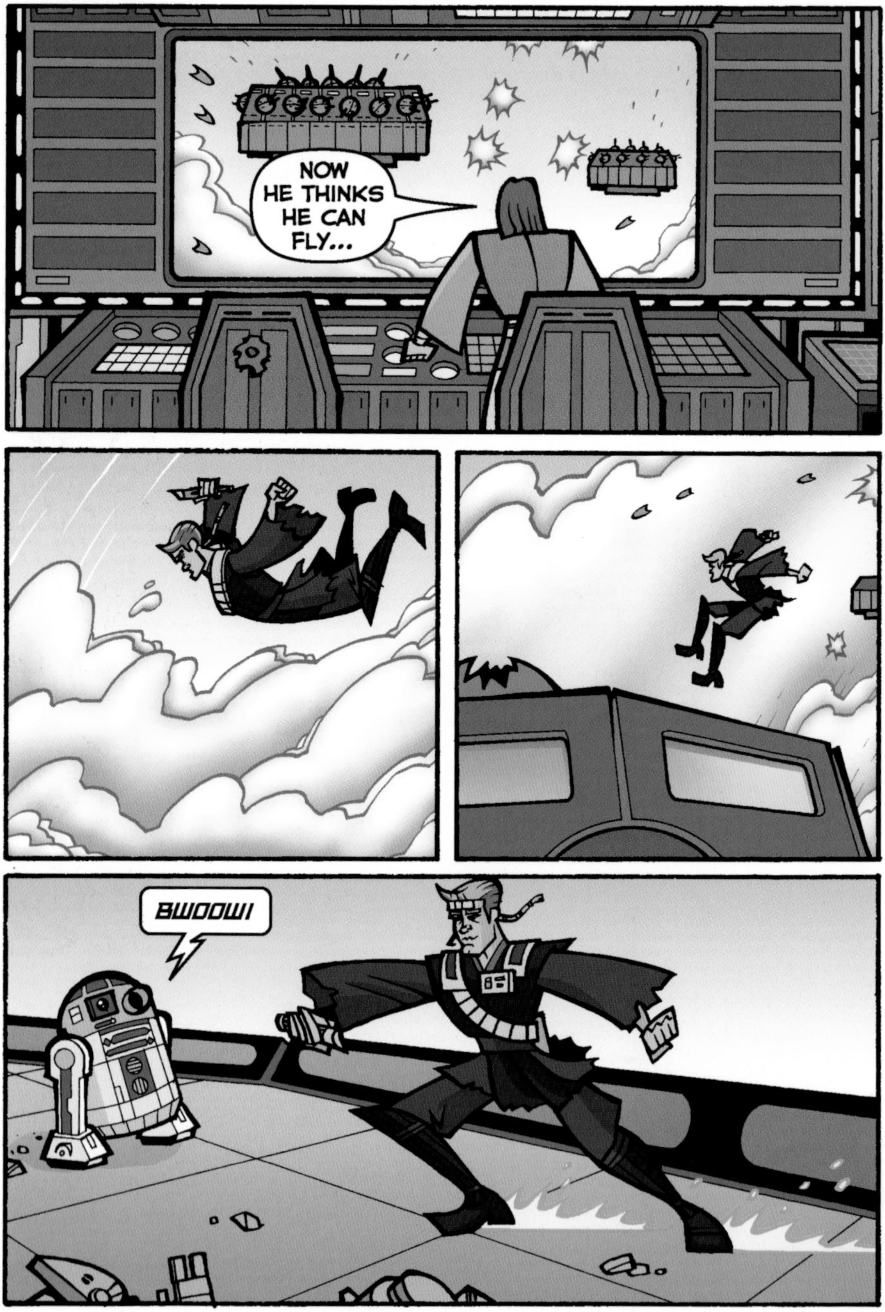
NOW HE THINKS HE CAN FLY...
BWOOWI

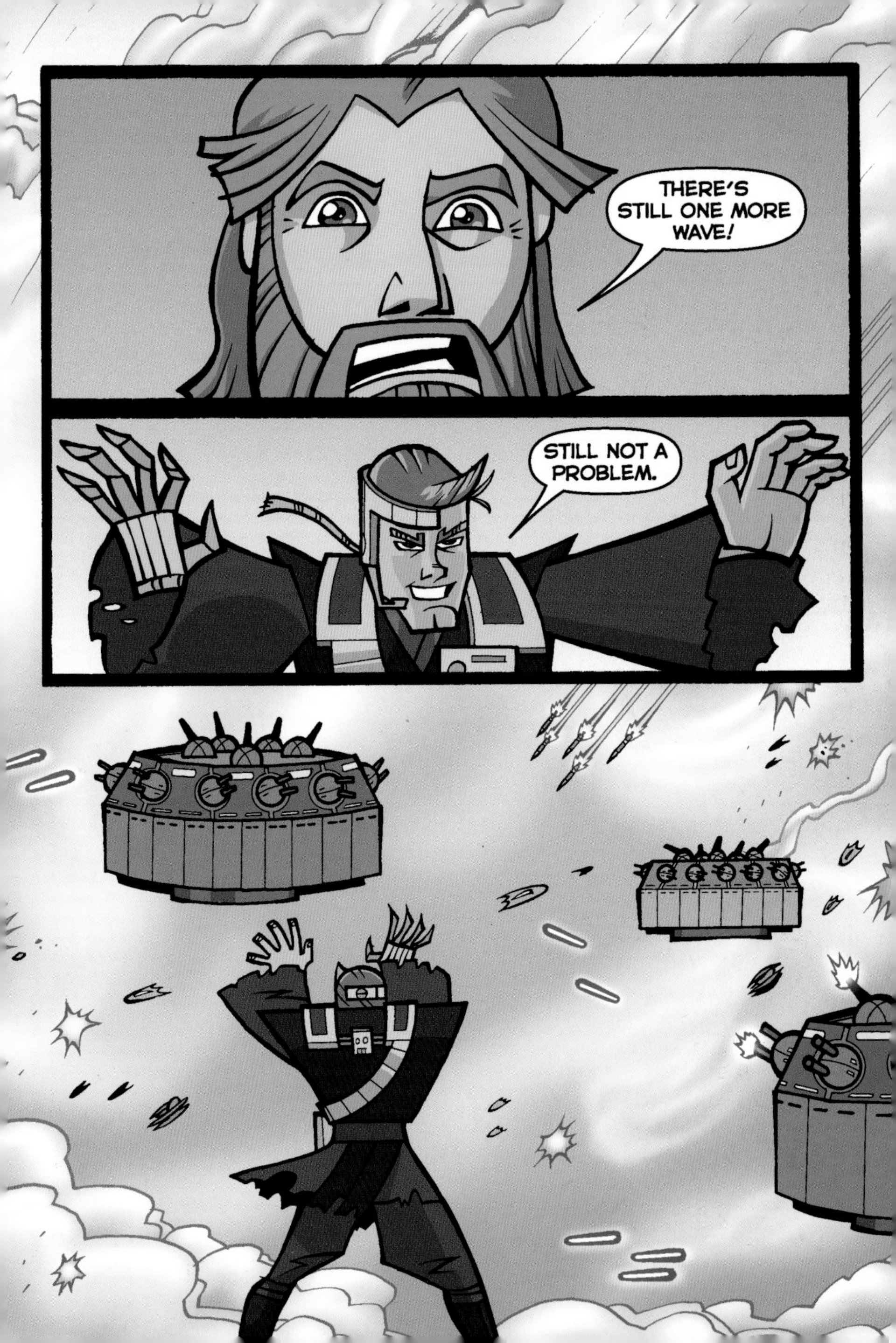
THERE'S STILL ONE MORE WAVE!
STILL NOT A PROBLEM.

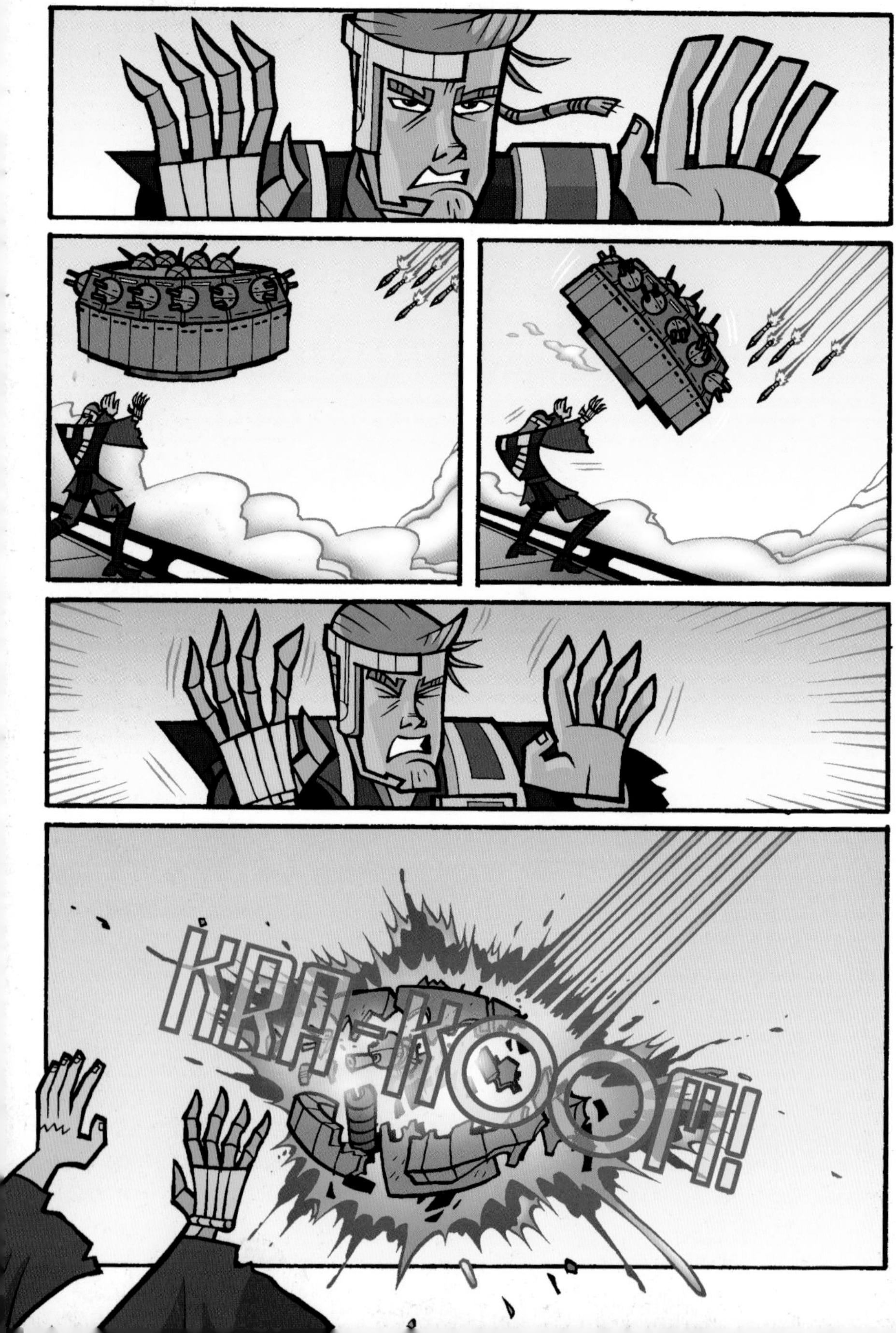
KRA-KOOM!

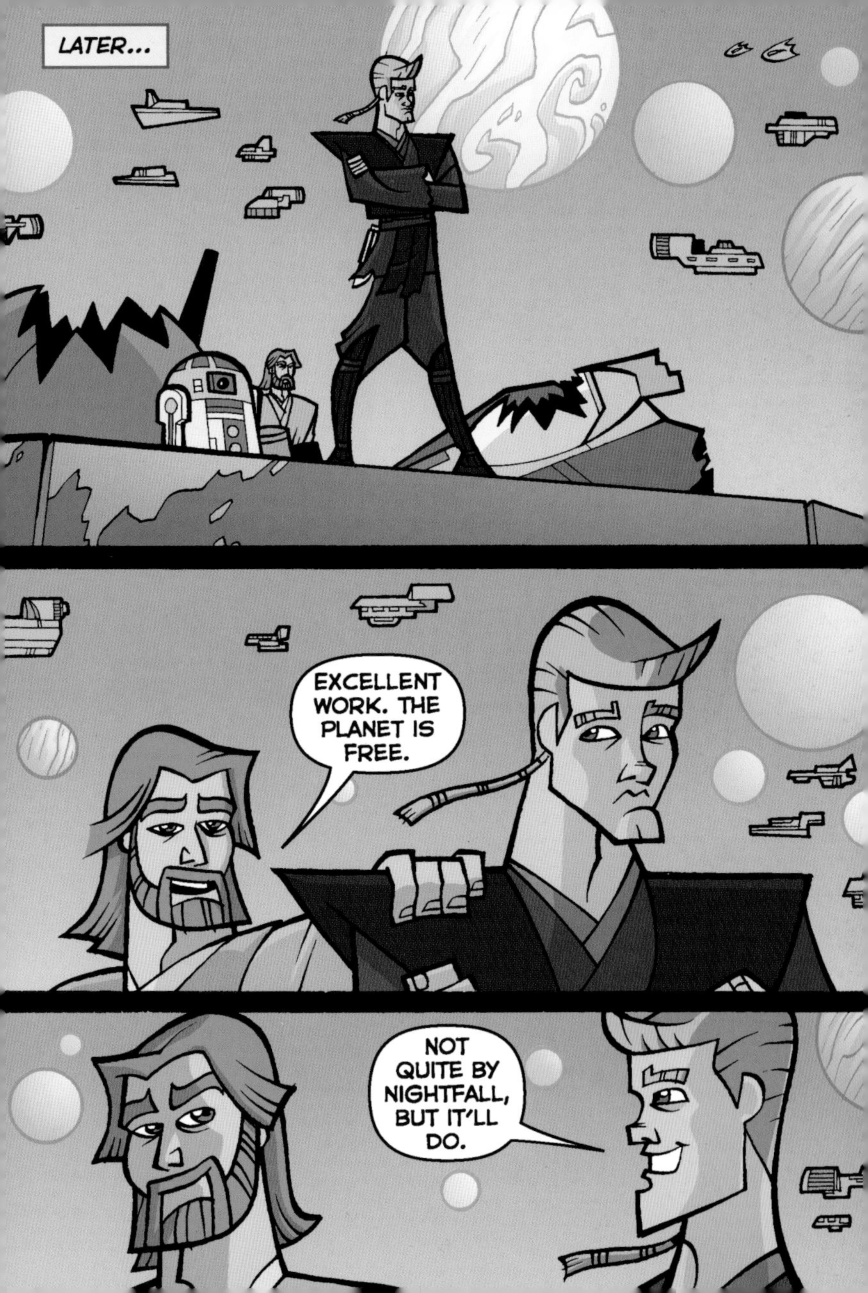
LATER...
EXCELLENT WORK. THE PLANET IS FREE.
NOT QUITE BY NIGHTFALL, BUT IT'LL DO.

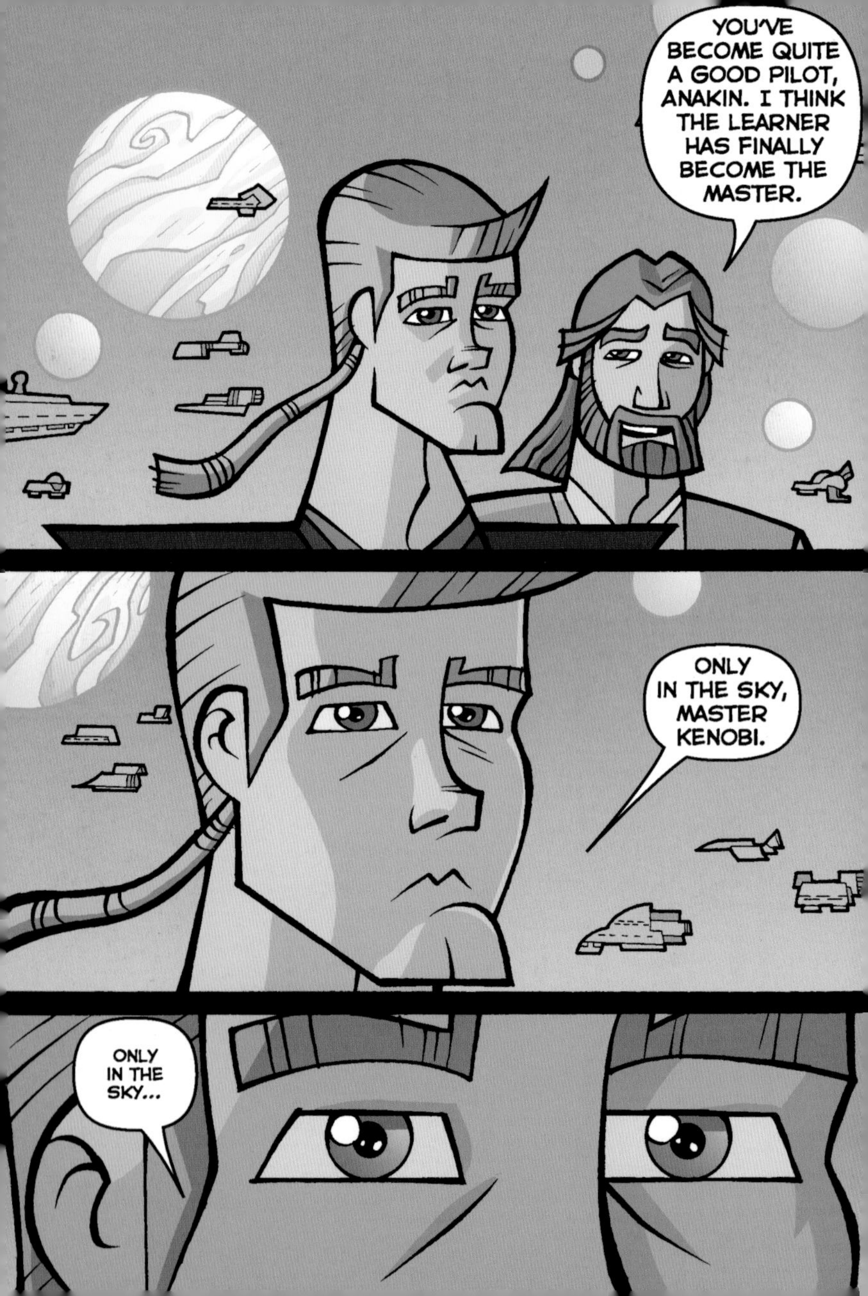
YOU'VE BECOME QUITE A GOOD PILOT, ANAKIN. I THINK THE LEARNER HAS FINALLY BECOME THE MASTER.
ONLY IN THE SKY, MASTER KENOBI.
ONLY IN THE SKY...

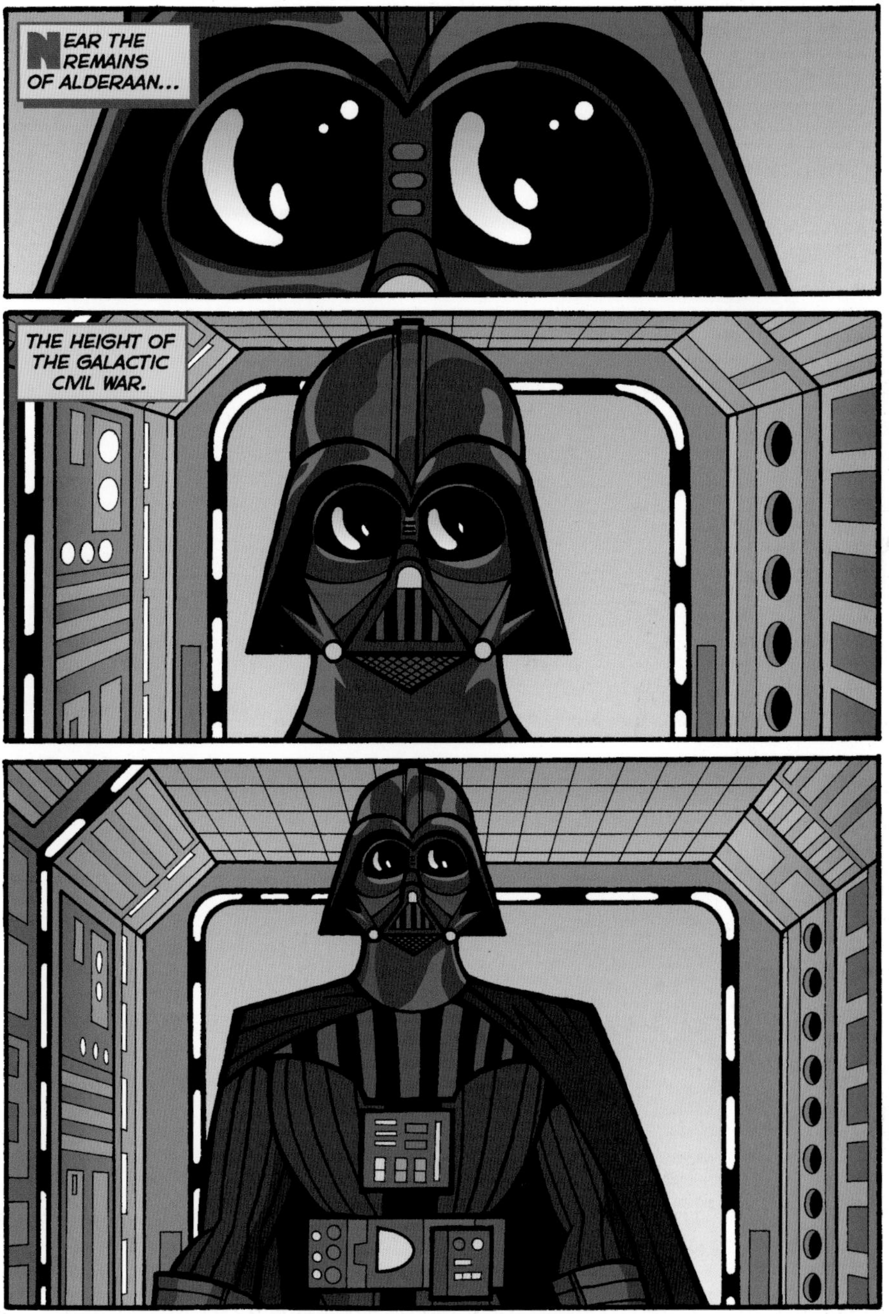
NEAR THE REMAINS OF ALDERAAN...
THE HEIGHT OF THE GALACTIC CIVIL WAR.

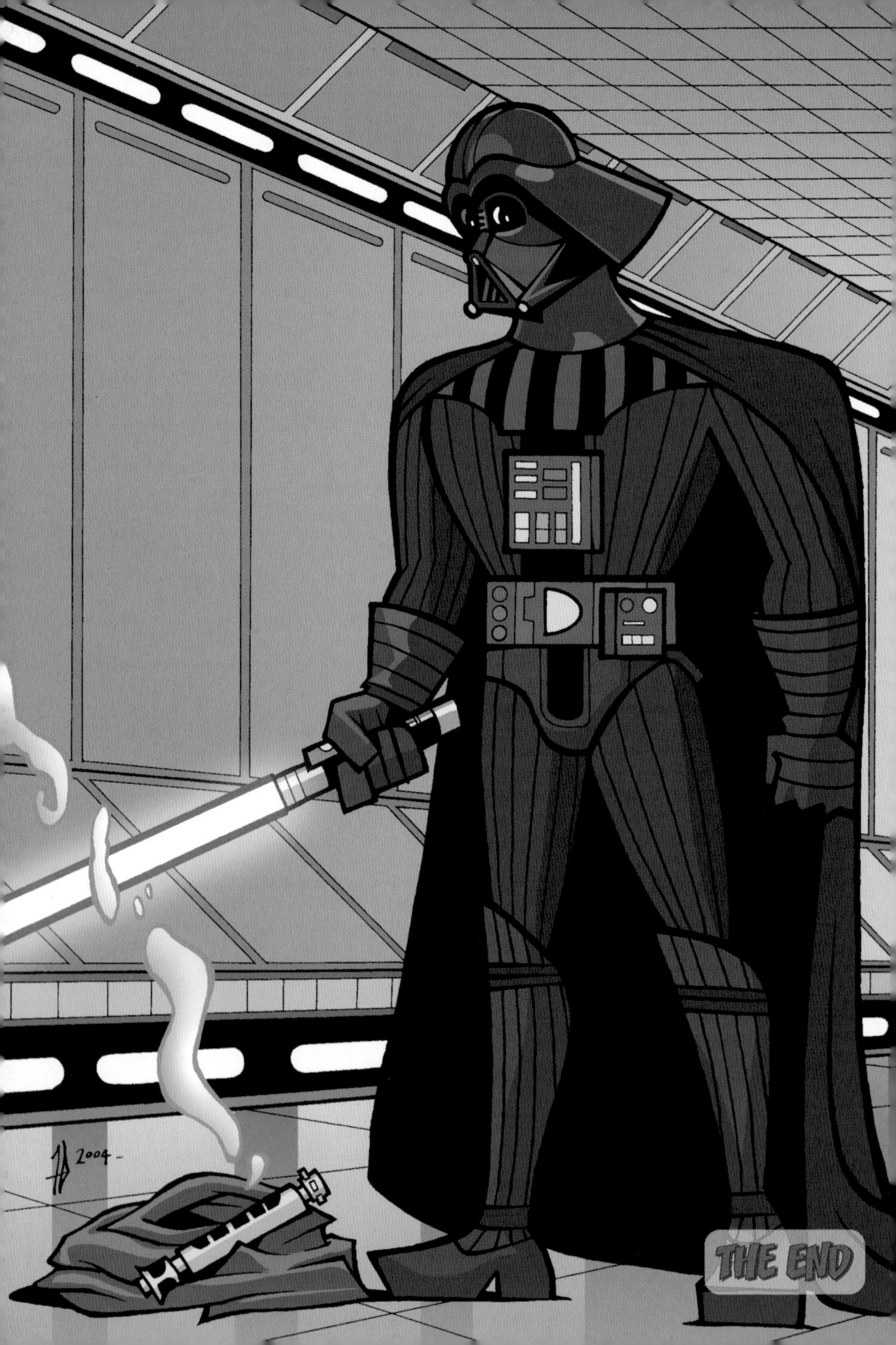
2004
THE END

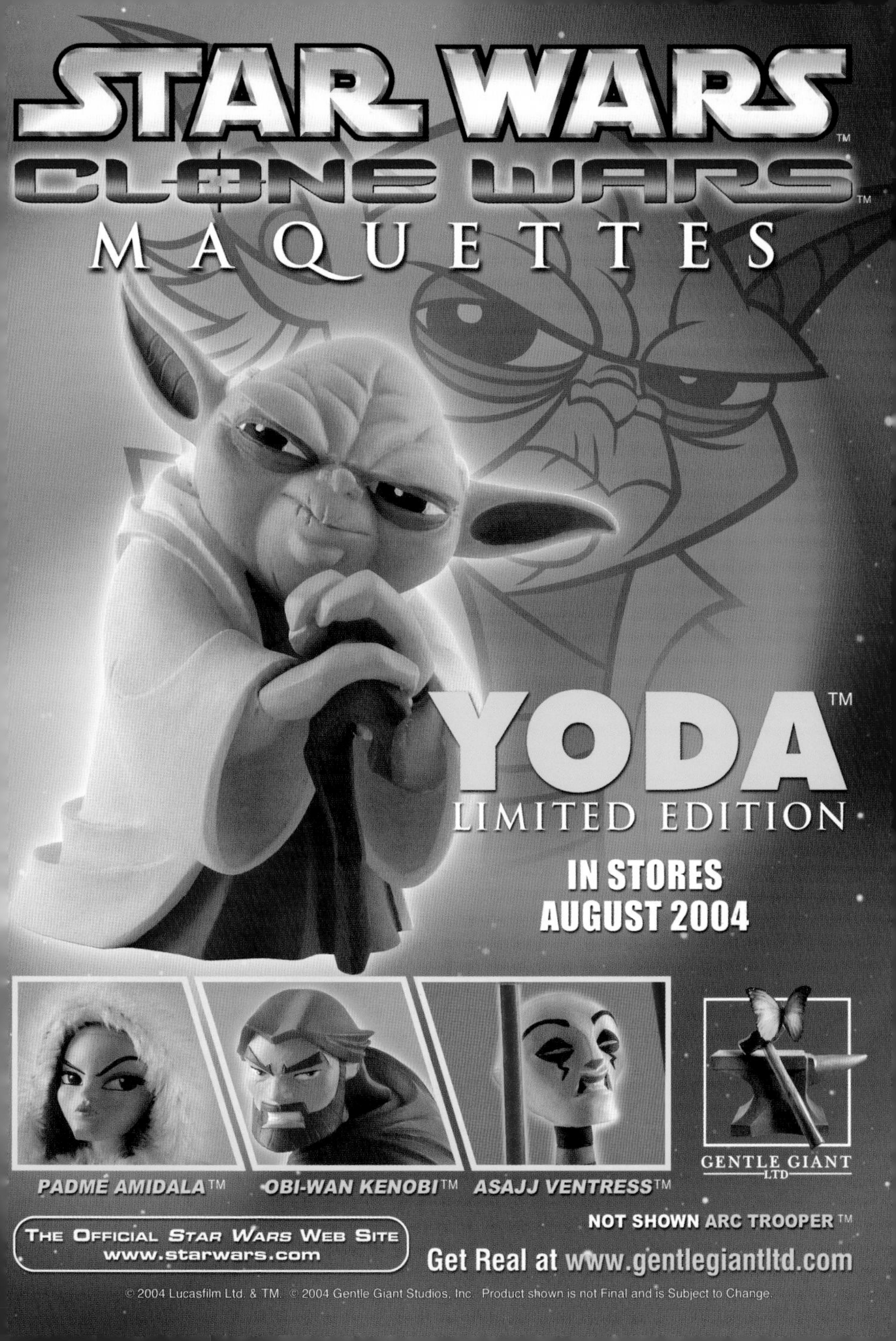

STAR WARS™
CLONE WARS™
MAQUETTES

YODA™
LIMITED EDITION

IN STORES
AUGUST 2004

PADMÉ AMIDALA™ **OBI-WAN KENOBI**™ **ASAJJ VENTRESS**™

GENTLE GIANT
LTD

NOT SHOWN ARC TROOPER™

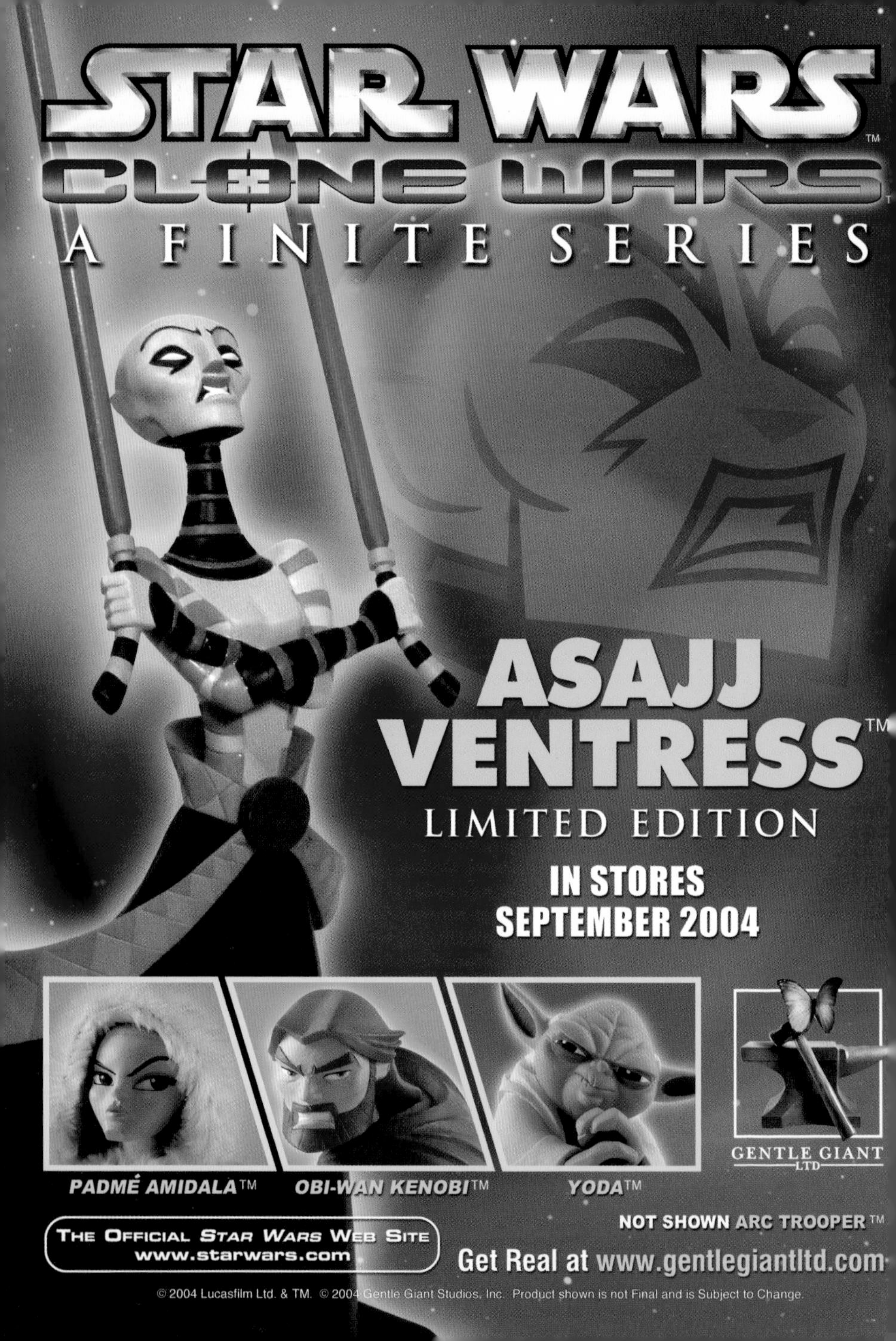

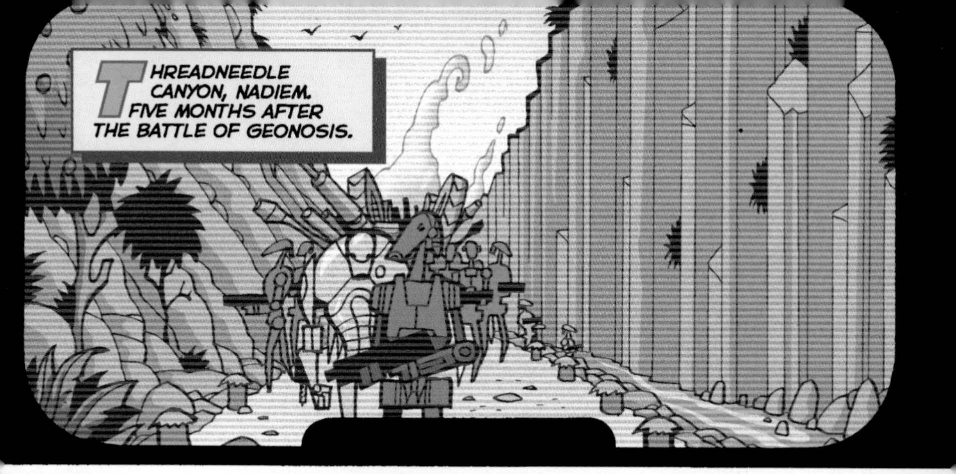
THREADNEEDLE CANYON, NADIEM. FIVE MONTHS AFTER THE BATTLE OF GEONOSIS.

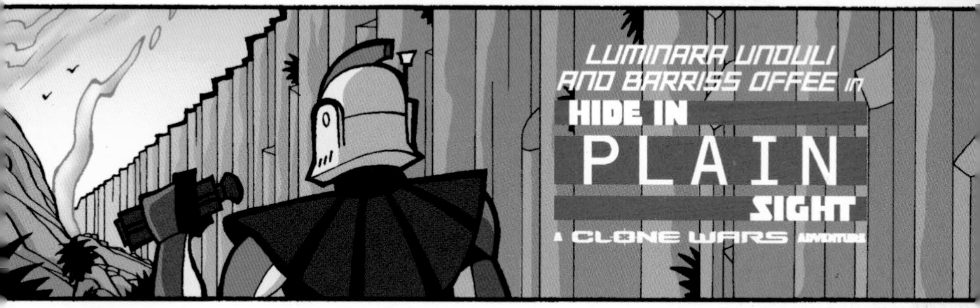
LUMINARA UNDULI AND BARRISS OFFEE IN
HIDE IN PLAIN SIGHT
A CLONE WARS ADVENTURE

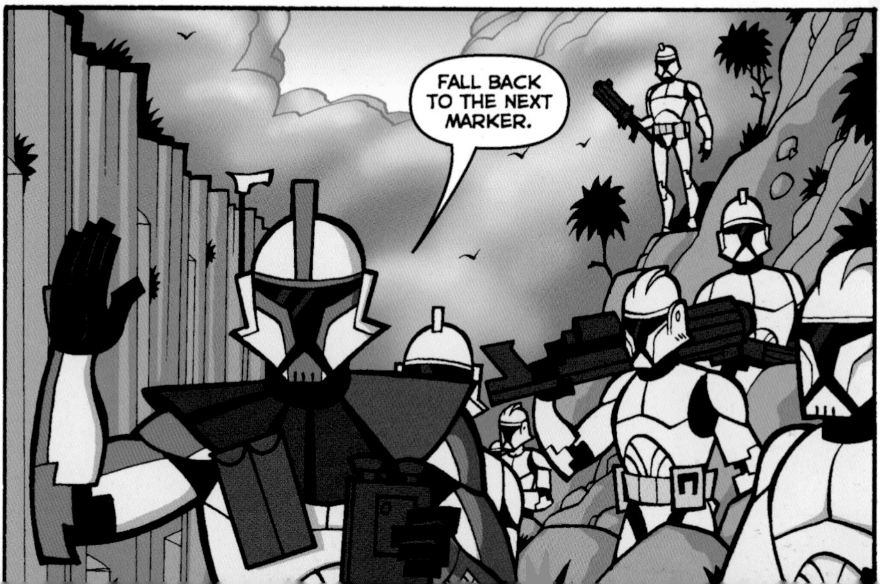
FALL BACK TO THE NEXT MARKER.
2004

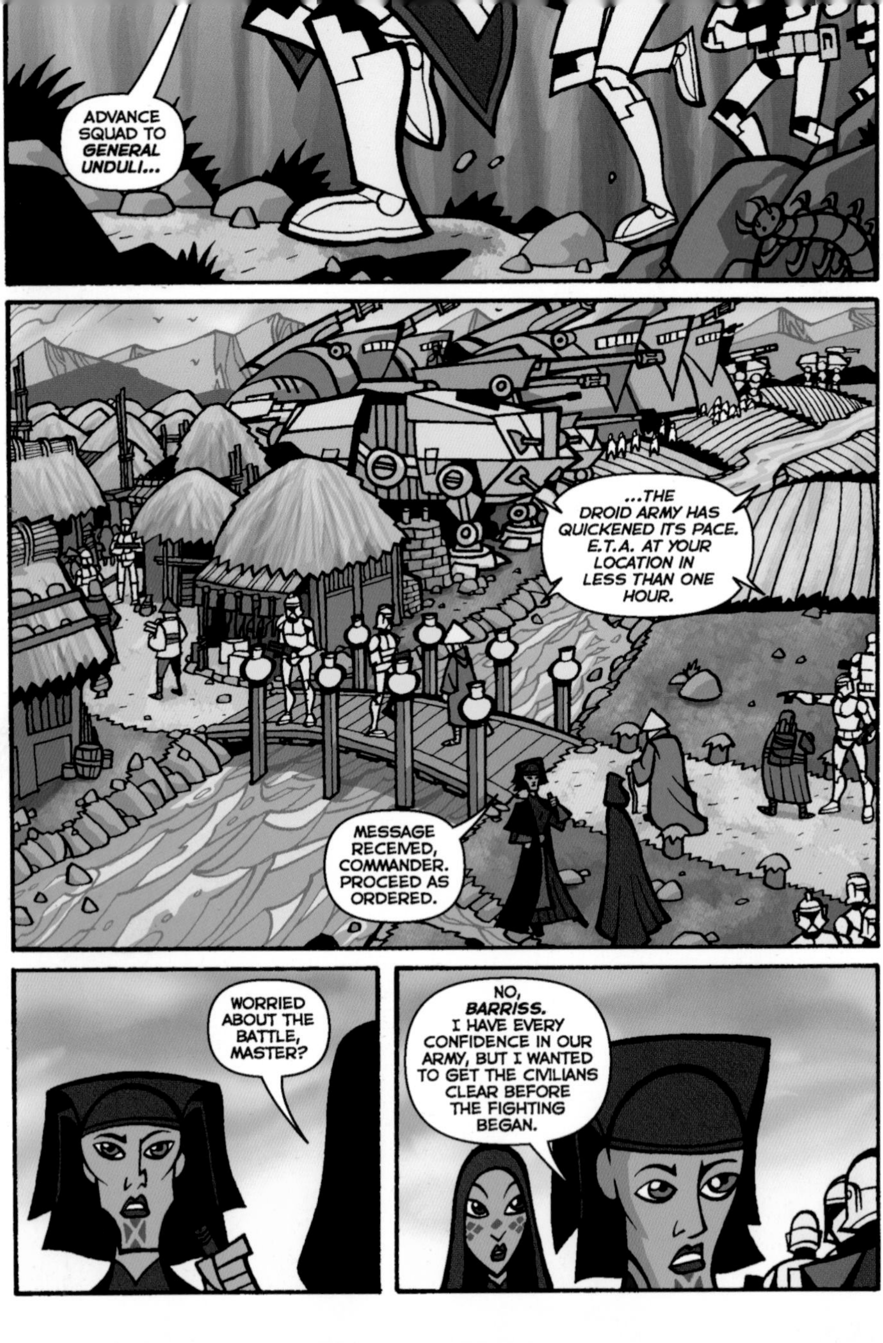
ADVANCE SQUAD TO GENERAL UNDULI...
...THE DROID ARMY HAS QUICKENED ITS PACE. E.T.A. AT YOUR LOCATION IN LESS THAN ONE HOUR.
MESSAGE RECEIVED, COMMANDER. PROCEED AS ORDERED.
WORRIED ABOUT THE BATTLE, MASTER?
NO, BARRISS. I HAVE EVERY CONFIDENCE IN OUR ARMY, BUT I WANTED TO GET THE CIVILIANS CLEAR BEFORE THE FIGHTING BEGAN.

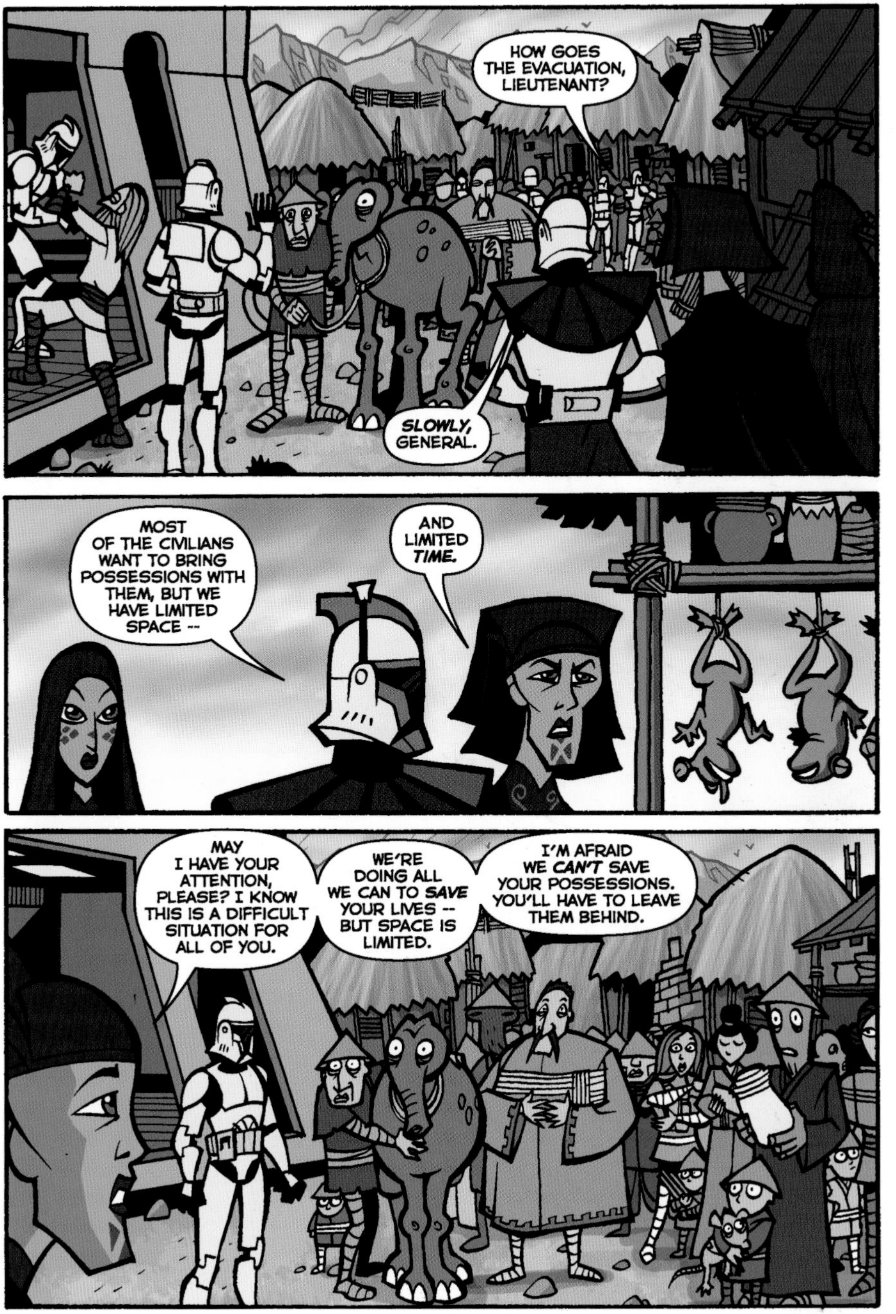
HOW GOES THE EVACUATION, LIEUTENANT?
SLOWLY, GENERAL.
MOST OF THE CIVILIANS WANT TO BRING POSSESSIONS WITH THEM, BUT WE HAVE LIMITED SPACE --
AND LIMITED TIME.
MAY I HAVE YOUR ATTENTION, PLEASE? I KNOW THIS IS A DIFFICULT SITUATION FOR ALL OF YOU.
WE'RE DOING ALL WE CAN TO SAVE YOUR LIVES -- BUT SPACE IS LIMITED.
I'M AFRAID WE CAN'T SAVE YOUR POSSESSIONS. YOU'LL HAVE TO LEAVE THEM BEHIND.

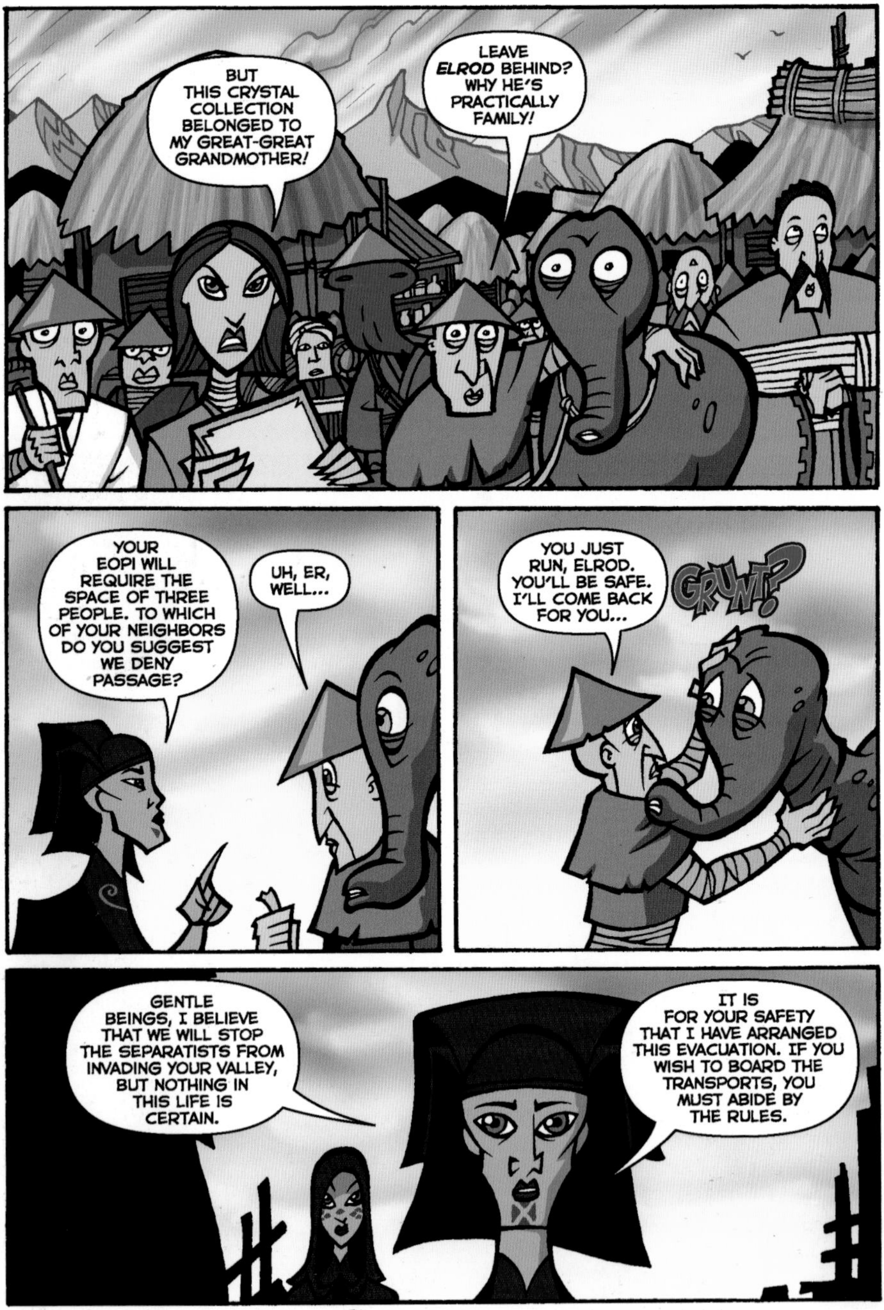
BUT THIS CRYSTAL COLLECTION BELONGED TO MY GREAT-GREAT GRANDMOTHER!
LEAVE ELROD BEHIND? WHY HE'S PRACTICALLY FAMILY!
YOUR EOPI WILL REQUIRE THE SPACE OF THREE PEOPLE. TO WHICH OF YOUR NEIGHBORS DO YOU SUGGEST WE DENY PASSAGE?
UH, ER, WELL...
YOU JUST RUN, ELROD. YOU'LL BE SAFE. I'LL COME BACK FOR YOU...
GRUNT?
GENTLE BEINGS, I BELIEVE THAT WE WILL STOP THE SEPARATISTS FROM INVADING YOUR VALLEY, BUT NOTHING IN THIS LIFE IS CERTAIN.
IT IS FOR YOUR SAFETY THAT I HAVE ARRANGED THIS EVACUATION. IF YOU WISH TO BOARD THE TRANSPORTS, YOU MUST ABIDE BY THE RULES.

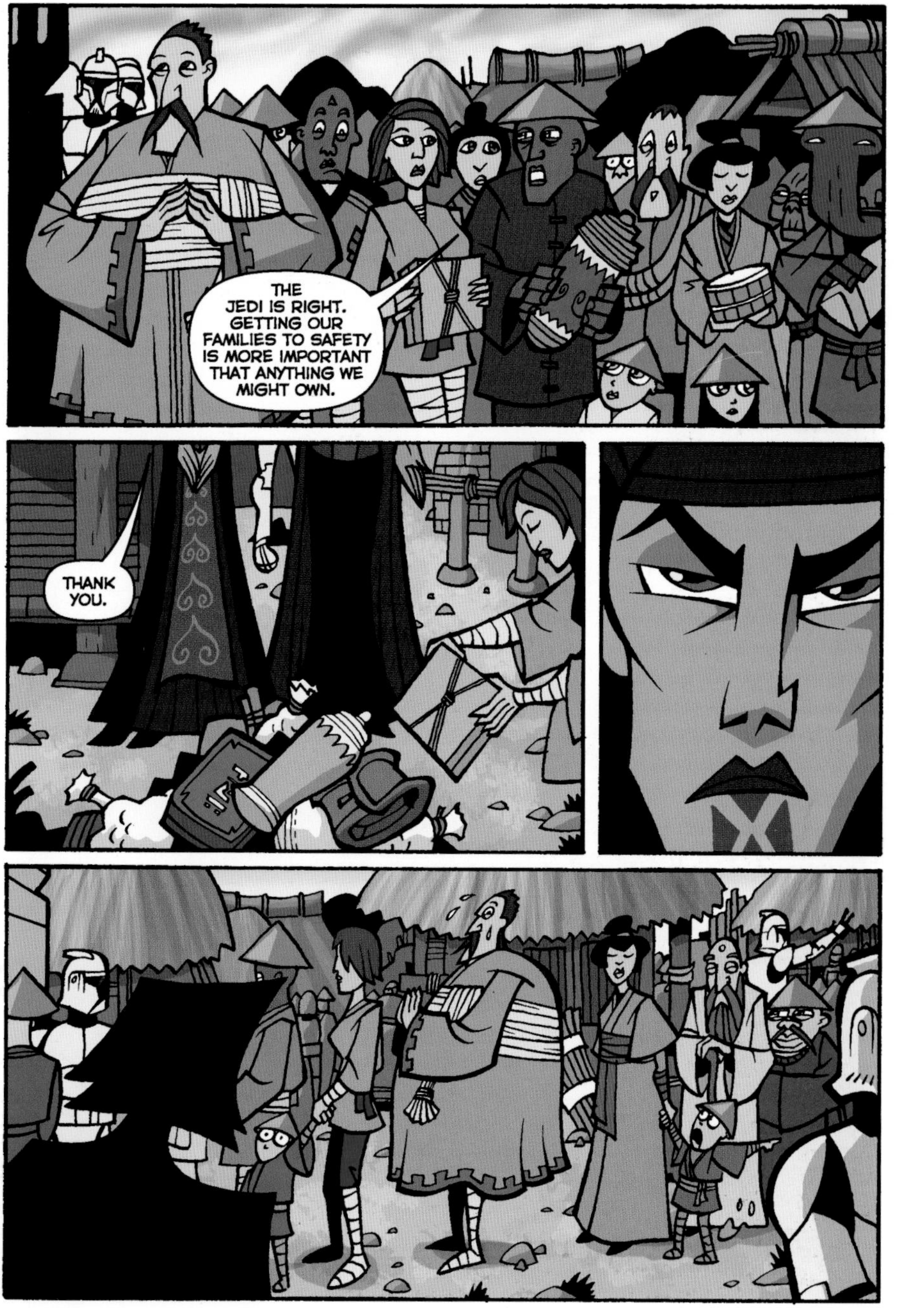
THE JEDI IS RIGHT. GETTING OUR FAMILIES TO SAFETY IS MORE IMPORTANT THAT ANYTHING WE MIGHT OWN.
THANK YOU.

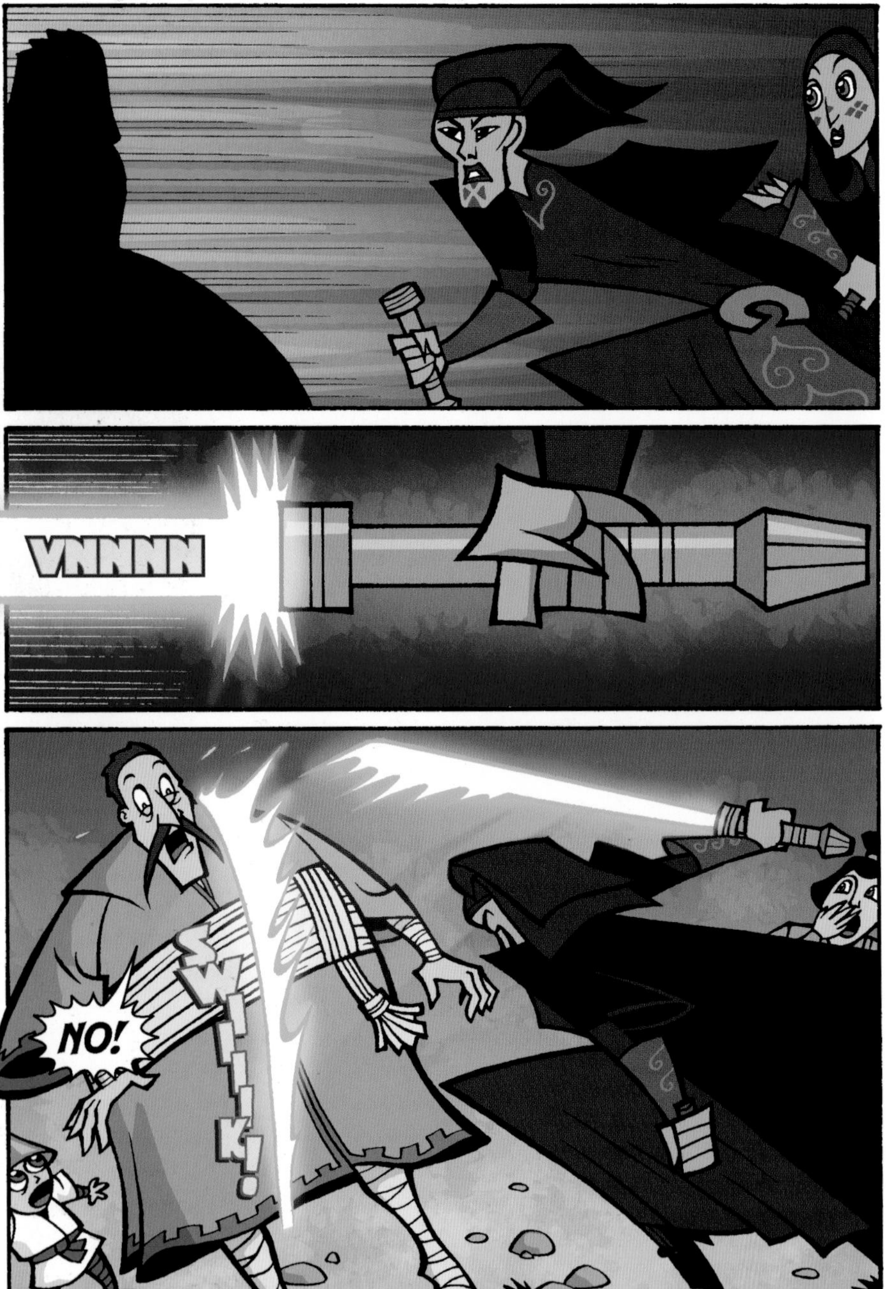
VNNNN
NO!
SWIIIIK!

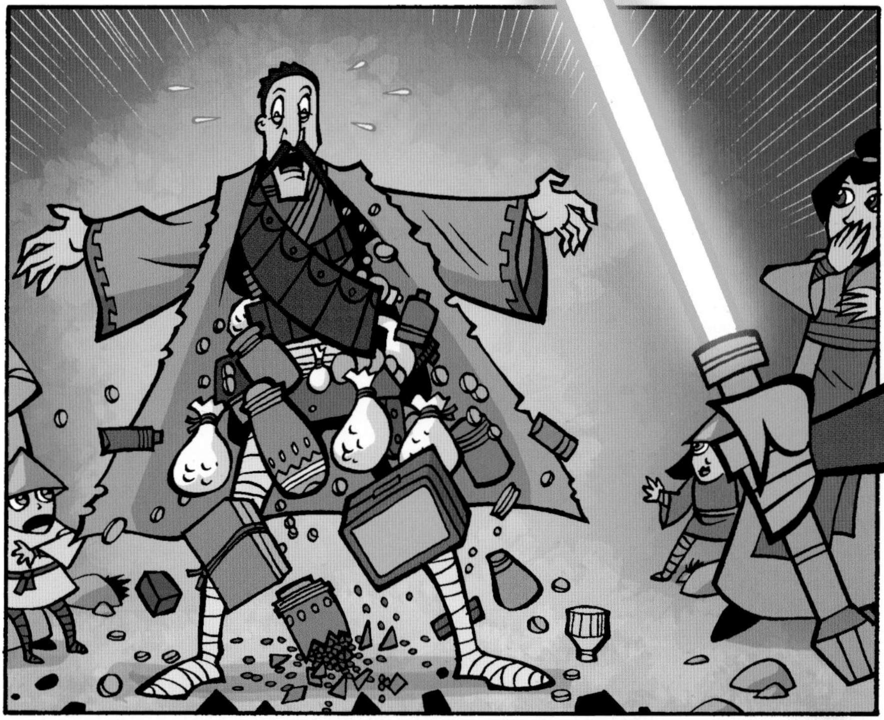

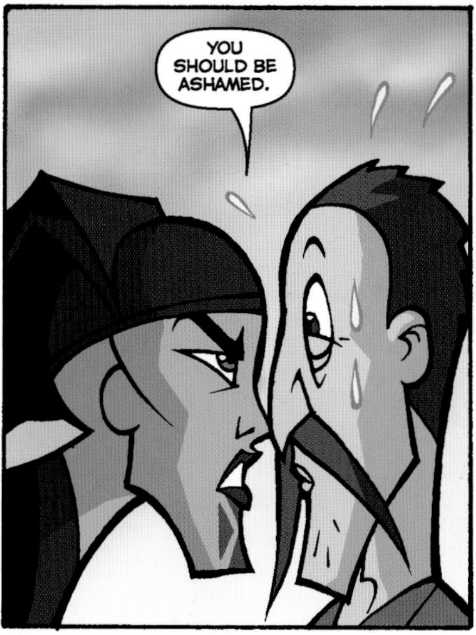
YOU SHOULD BE ASHAMED.

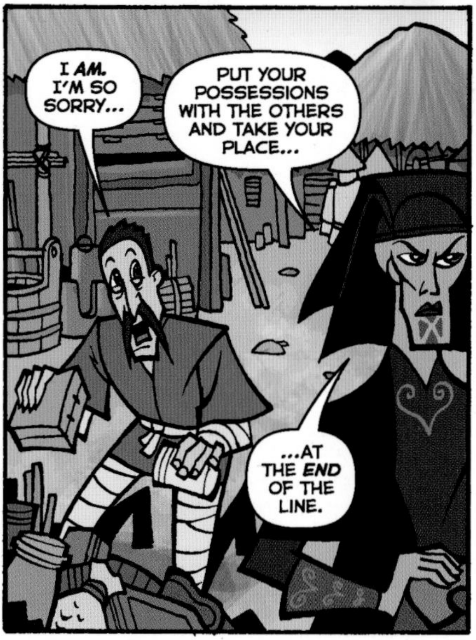
I *AM.* I'M SO SORRY...
PUT YOUR POSSESSIONS WITH THE OTHERS AND TAKE YOUR PLACE...
...AT THE *END* OF THE LINE.

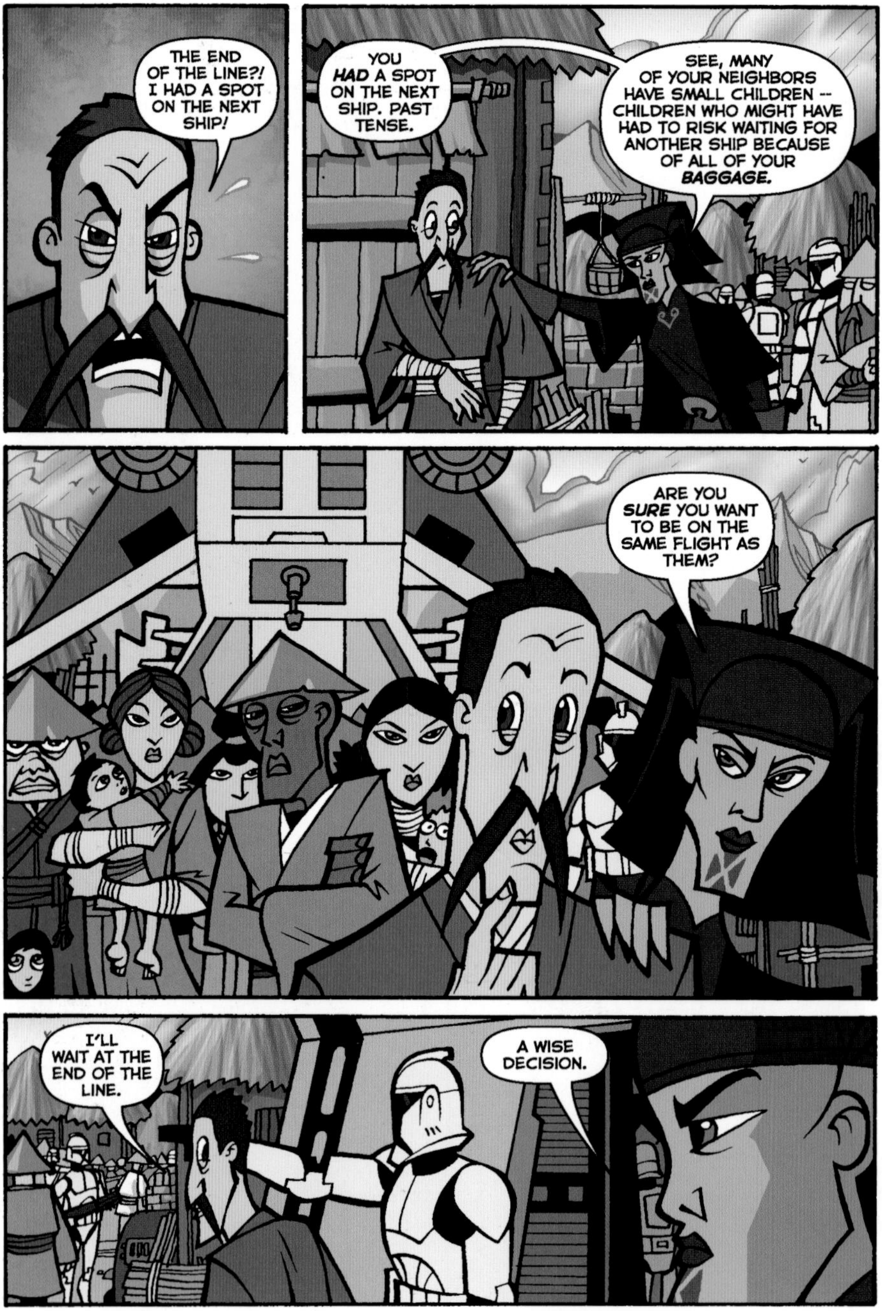
THE END OF THE LINE?! I HAD A SPOT ON THE NEXT SHIP!
YOU *HAD* A SPOT ON THE NEXT SHIP. PAST TENSE.
SEE, MANY OF YOUR NEIGHBORS HAVE SMALL CHILDREN -- CHILDREN WHO MIGHT HAVE HAD TO RISK WAITING FOR ANOTHER SHIP BECAUSE OF ALL OF YOUR *BAGGAGE.*
ARE YOU *SURE* YOU WANT TO BE ON THE SAME FLIGHT AS THEM?
I'LL WAIT AT THE END OF THE LINE.
A WISE DECISION.

HOW DID YOU KNOW HE WAS HIDING SOMETHING?

BECAUSE HE WAS THE *ONLY* PERSON IN LINE *NOT* CARRYING SOMETHING.

SOMETIMES TRYING TOO HARD TO ESCAPE DETECTION WILL DRAW ATTENTION TO ONE'S SELF.

BESIDES, FOR A MAN OF HIS APPARENT GIRTH, HE HAD AWFULLY SKINNY LEGS!

GENERAL -- !

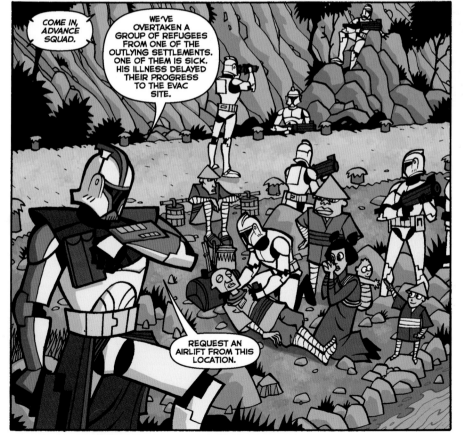

COME IN, ADVANCE SQUAD.

WE'VE OVERTAKEN A GROUP OF REFUGEES FROM ONE OF THE OUTLYING SETTLEMENTS. ONE OF THEM IS SICK. HIS ILLNESS DELAYED THEIR PROGRESS TO THE EVAC SITE.

REQUEST AN AIRLIFT FROM THIS LOCATION.

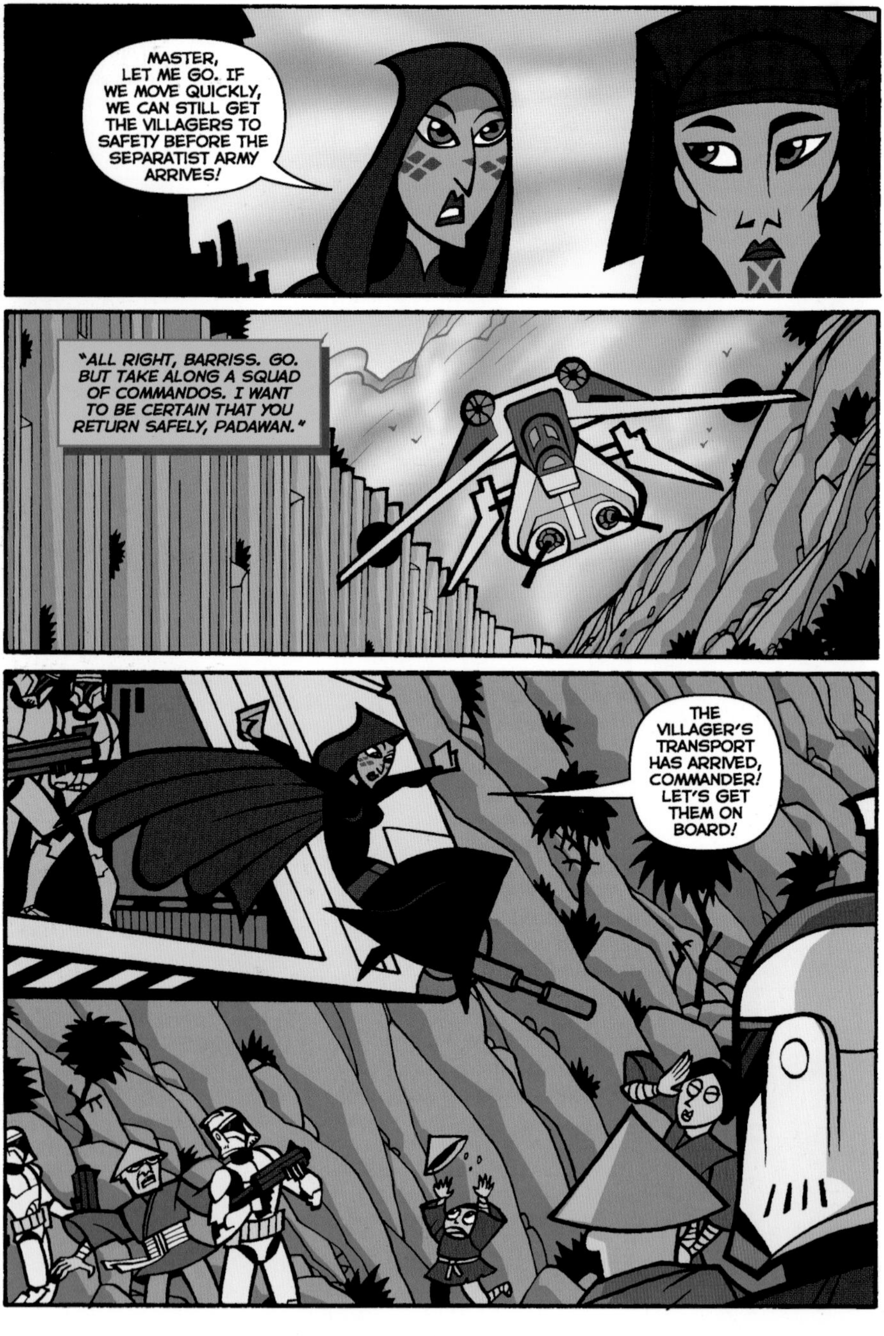
MASTER, LET ME GO. IF WE MOVE QUICKLY, WE CAN STILL GET THE VILLAGERS TO SAFETY BEFORE THE SEPARATIST ARMY ARRIVES!
"ALL RIGHT, BARRISS. GO. BUT TAKE ALONG A SQUAD OF COMMANDOS. I WANT TO BE CERTAIN THAT YOU RETURN SAFELY, PADAWAN."
THE VILLAGER'S TRANSPORT HAS ARRIVED, COMMANDER! LET'S GET THEM ON BOARD!

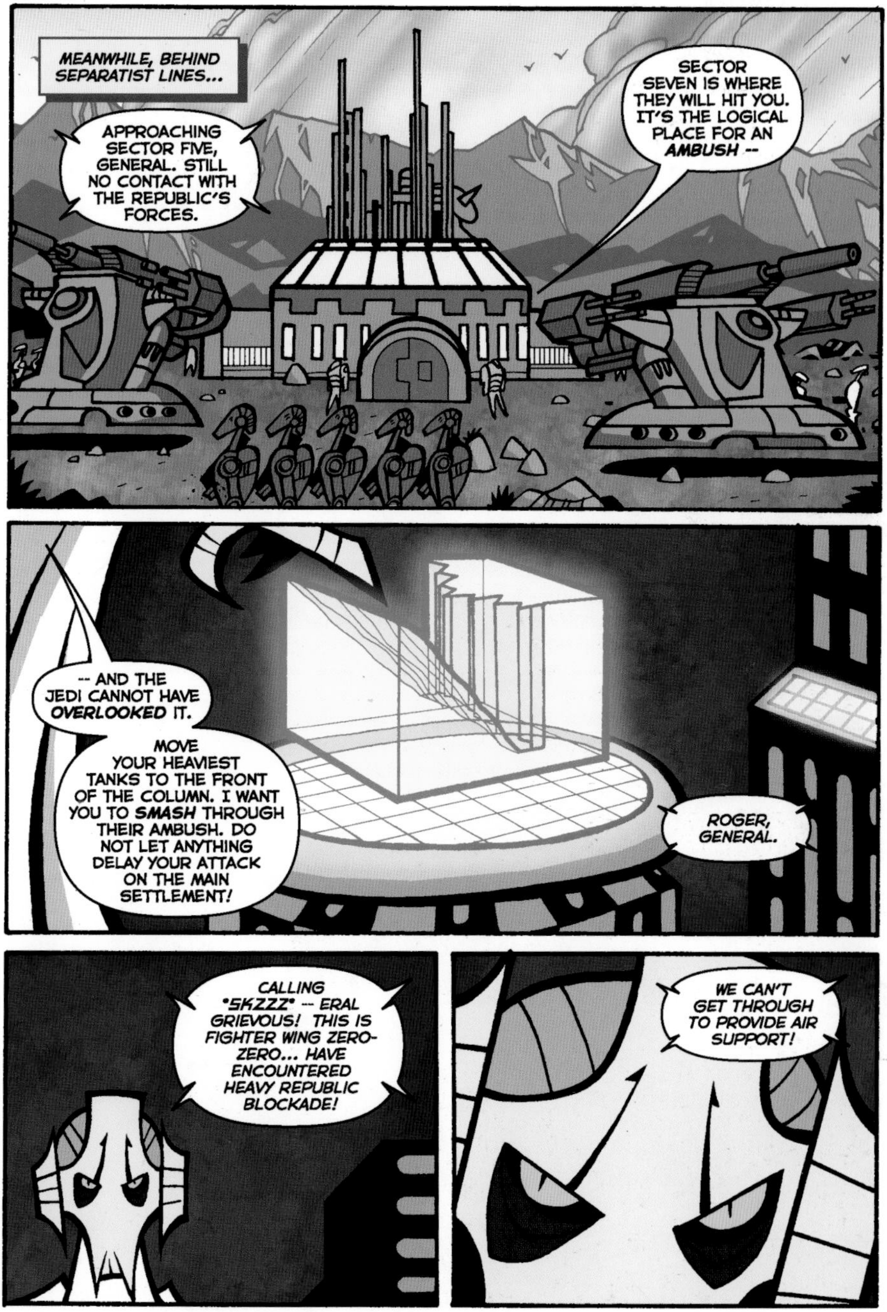
MEANWHILE, BEHIND SEPARATIST LINES...
APPROACHING SECTOR FIVE, GENERAL. STILL NO CONTACT WITH THE REPUBLIC'S FORCES.
SECTOR SEVEN IS WHERE THEY WILL HIT YOU. IT'S THE LOGICAL PLACE FOR AN AMBUSH --
-- AND THE JEDI CANNOT HAVE OVERLOOKED IT.
MOVE YOUR HEAVIEST TANKS TO THE FRONT OF THE COLUMN. I WANT YOU TO SMASH THROUGH THEIR AMBUSH. DO NOT LET ANYTHING DELAY YOUR ATTACK ON THE MAIN SETTLEMENT!
ROGER, GENERAL.
CALLING *SKZZZ* -- ERAL GRIEVOUS! THIS IS FIGHTER WING ZERO-ZERO... HAVE ENCOUNTERED HEAVY REPUBLIC BLOCKADE!
WE CAN'T GET THROUGH TO PROVIDE AIR SUPPORT!

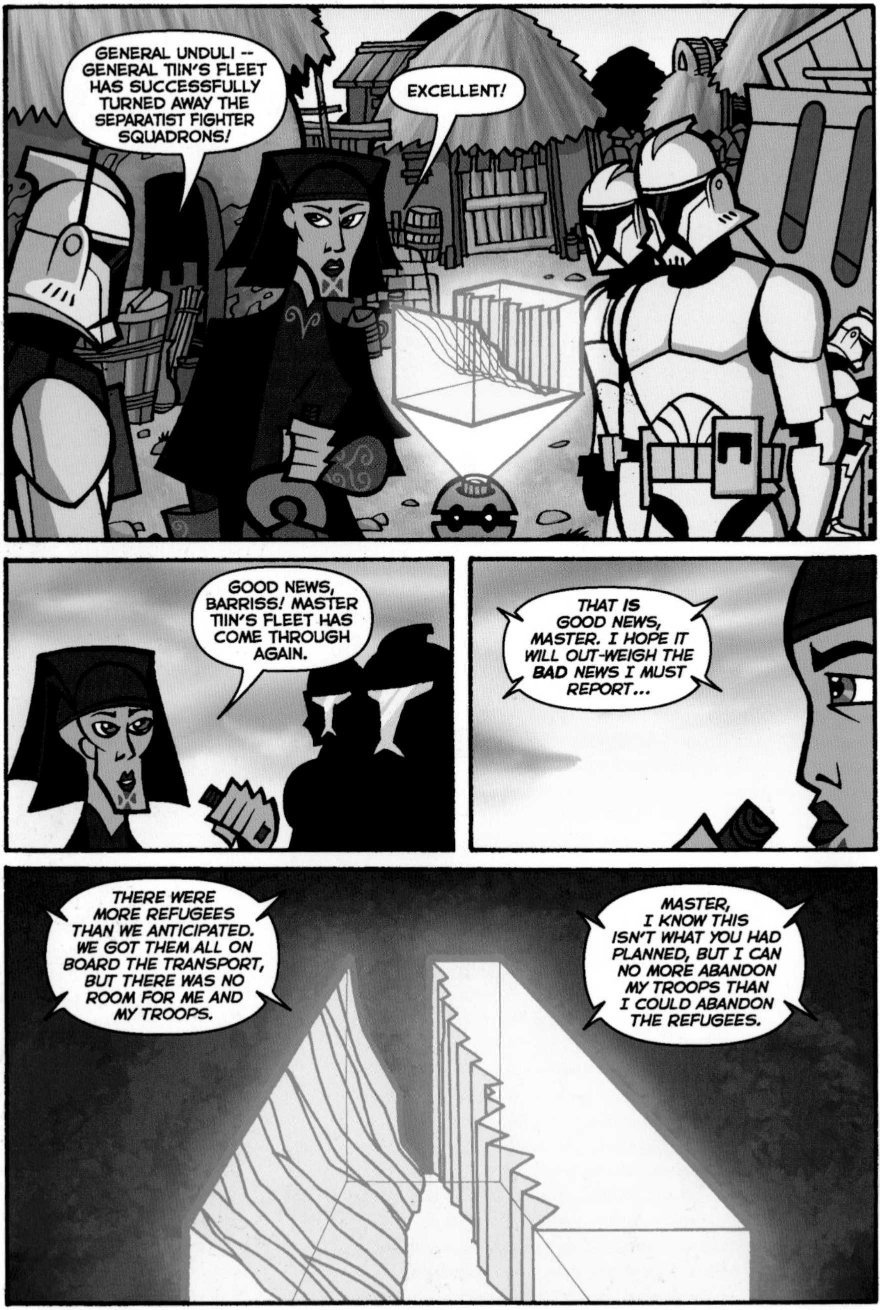
GENERAL UNDULI -- GENERAL TIIN'S FLEET HAS SUCCESSFULLY TURNED AWAY THE SEPARATIST FIGHTER SQUADRONS!
EXCELLENT!
GOOD NEWS, BARRISS! MASTER TIIN'S FLEET HAS COME THROUGH AGAIN.
THAT IS GOOD NEWS, MASTER. I HOPE IT WILL OUT-WEIGH THE BAD NEWS I MUST REPORT...
THERE WERE MORE REFUGEES THAN WE ANTICIPATED. WE GOT THEM ALL ON BOARD THE TRANSPORT, BUT THERE WAS NO ROOM FOR ME AND MY TROOPS.
MASTER, I KNOW THIS ISN'T WHAT YOU HAD PLANNED, BUT I CAN NO MORE ABANDON MY TROOPS THAN I COULD ABANDON THE REFUGEES.

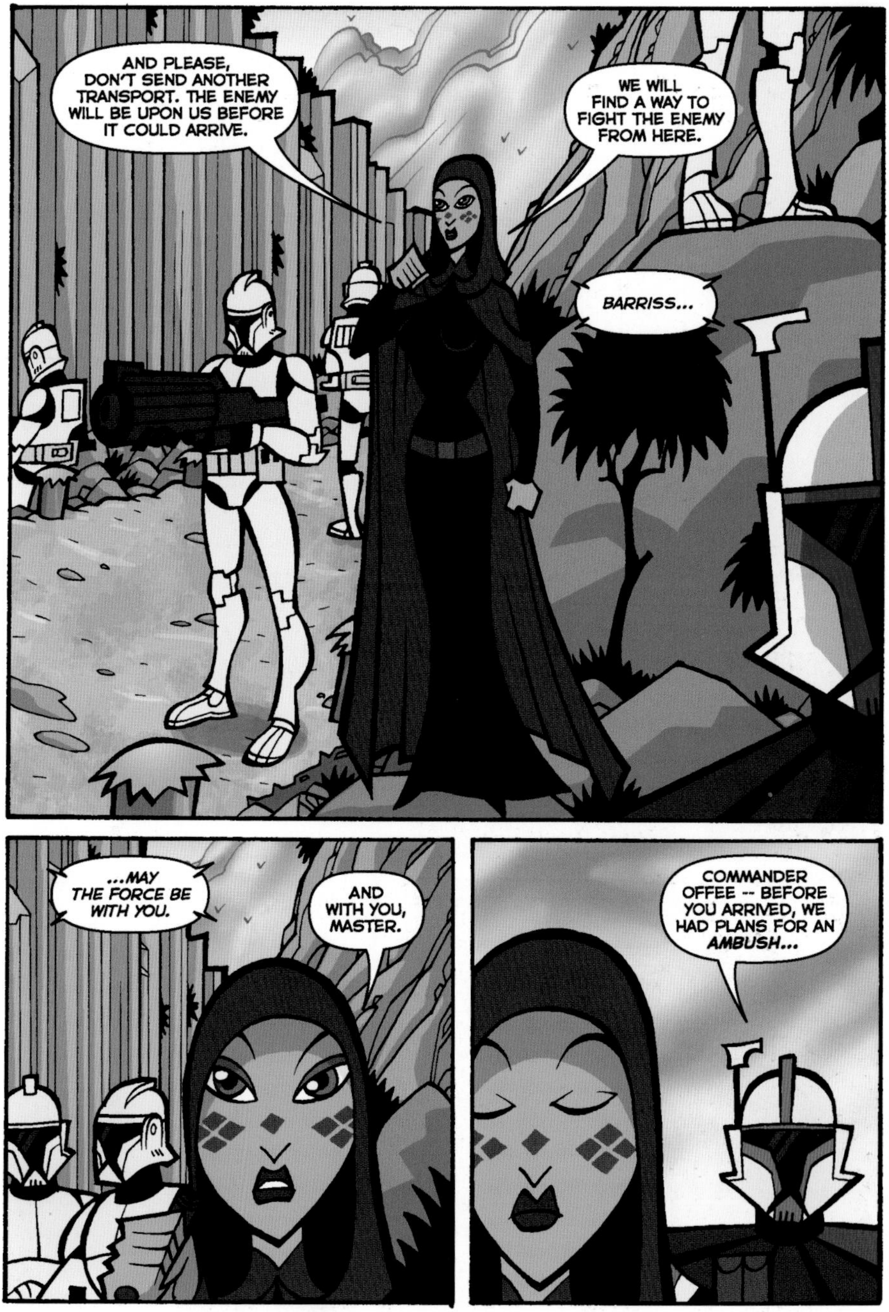
AND PLEASE, DON'T SEND ANOTHER TRANSPORT. THE ENEMY WILL BE UPON US BEFORE IT COULD ARRIVE.
WE WILL FIND A WAY TO FIGHT THE ENEMY FROM HERE.
BARRISS...
...MAY THE FORCE BE WITH YOU.
AND WITH YOU, MASTER.
COMMANDER OFFEE -- BEFORE YOU ARRIVED, WE HAD PLANS FOR AN AMBUSH...

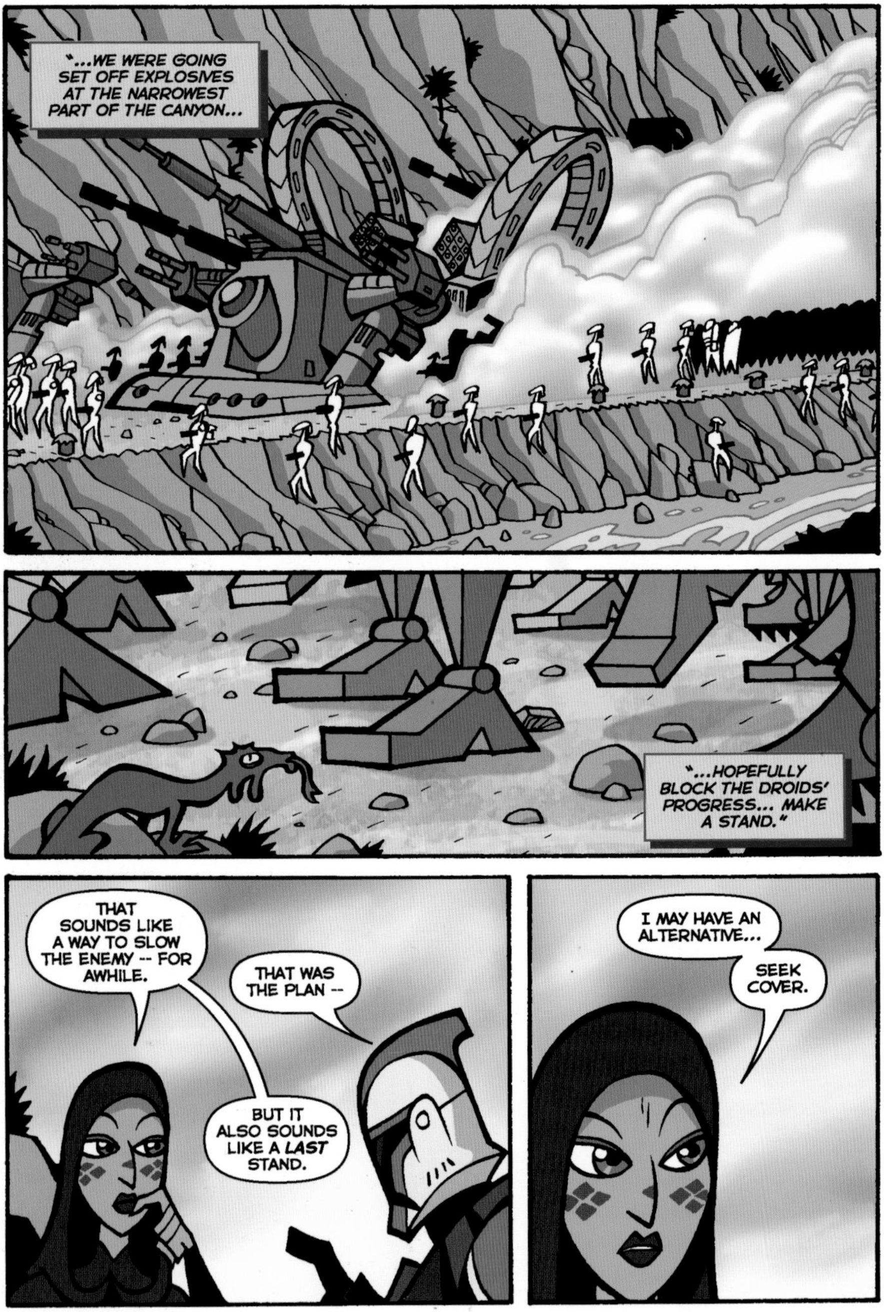
"...WE WERE GOING SET OFF EXPLOSIVES AT THE NARROWEST PART OF THE CANYON...
"...HOPEFULLY BLOCK THE DROIDS' PROGRESS... MAKE A STAND."
THAT SOUNDS LIKE A WAY TO SLOW THE ENEMY -- FOR AWHILE.
THAT WAS THE PLAN --
BUT IT ALSO SOUNDS LIKE A *LAST* STAND.
I MAY HAVE AN ALTERNATIVE...
SEEK COVER.

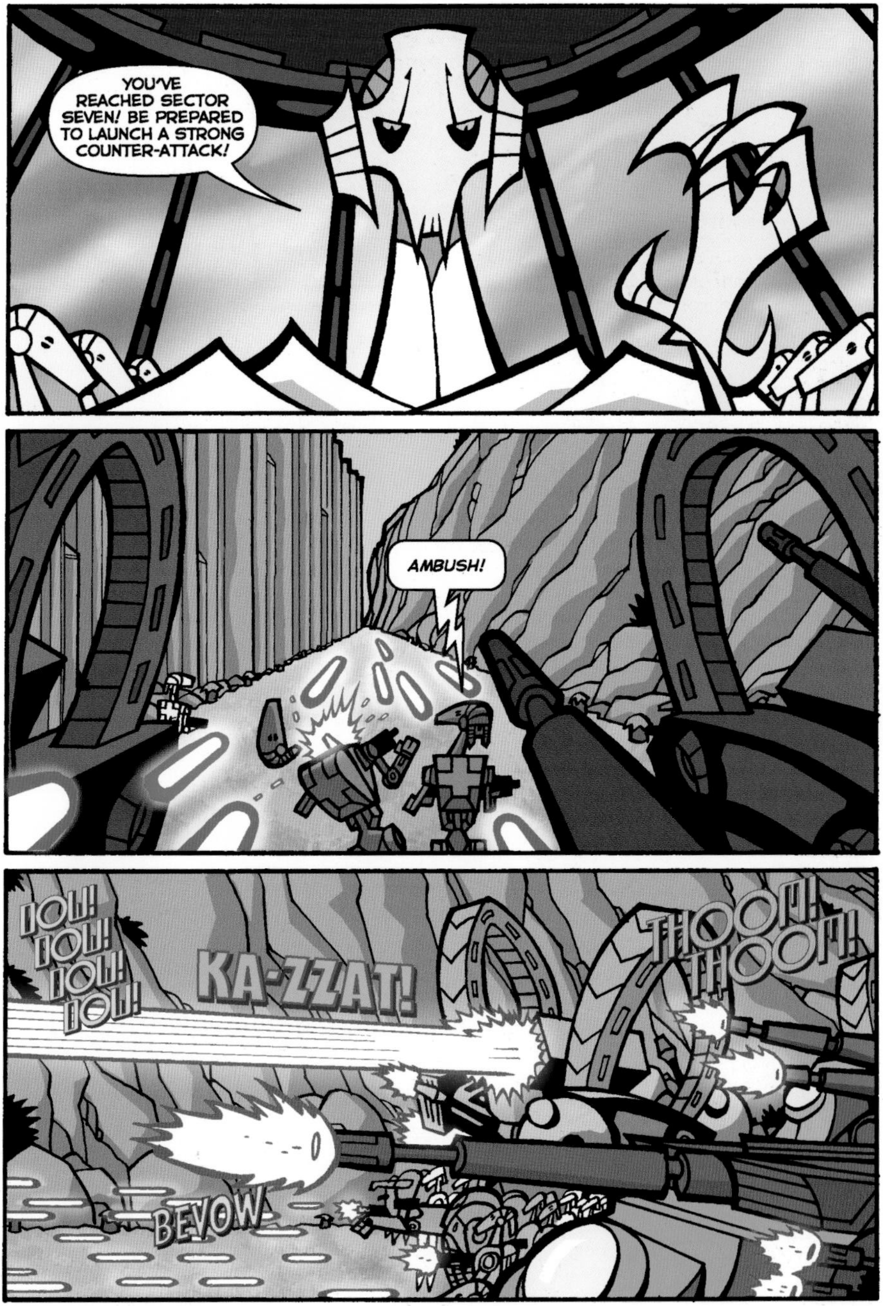
YOU'VE REACHED SECTOR SEVEN! BE PREPARED TO LAUNCH A STRONG COUNTER-ATTACK!
AMBUSH!
DOW! DOW! DOW! DOW!
KA-ZZAT!
THOOM! THOOM!
BEVOW

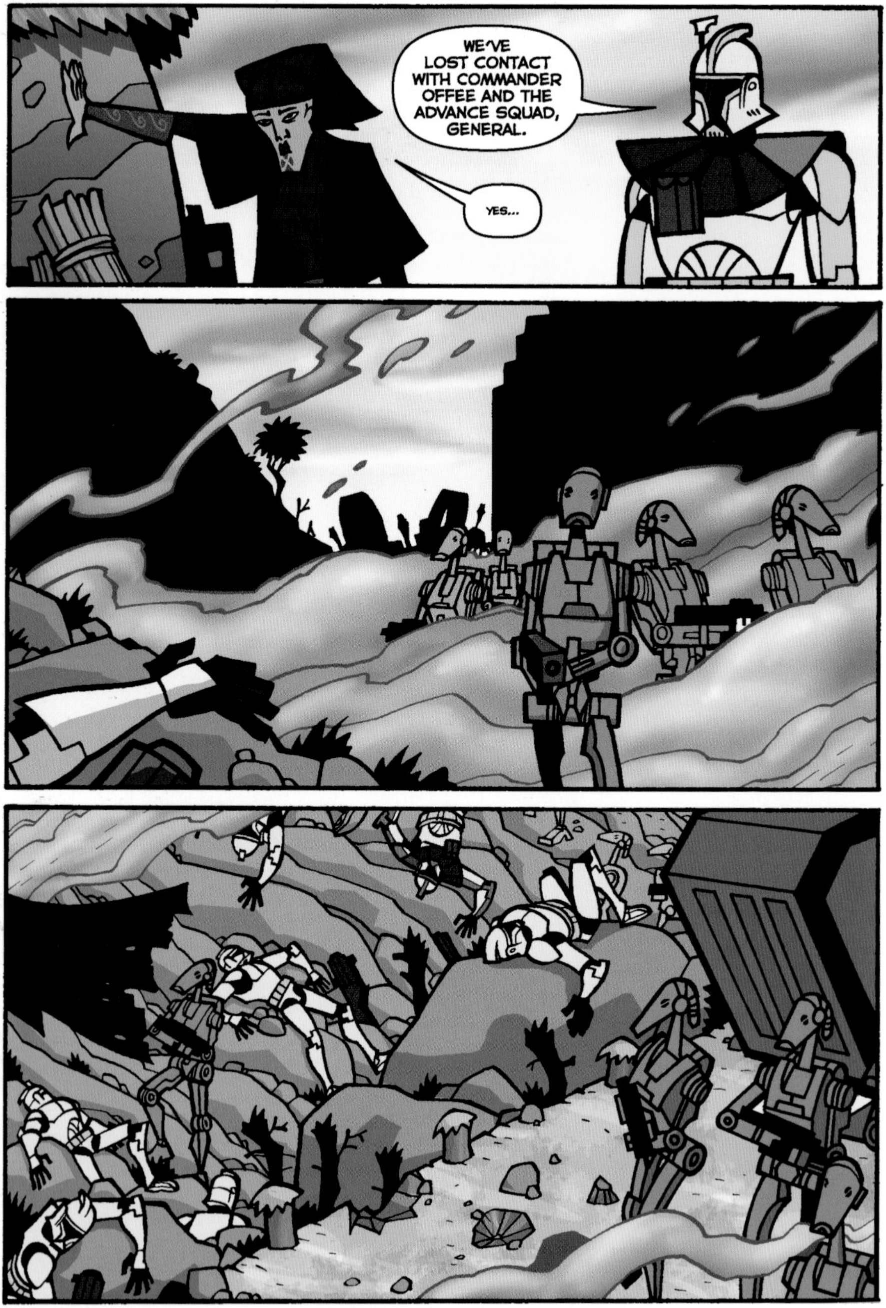
WE'VE LOST CONTACT WITH COMMANDER OFFEE AND THE ADVANCE SQUAD, GENERAL.
YES...

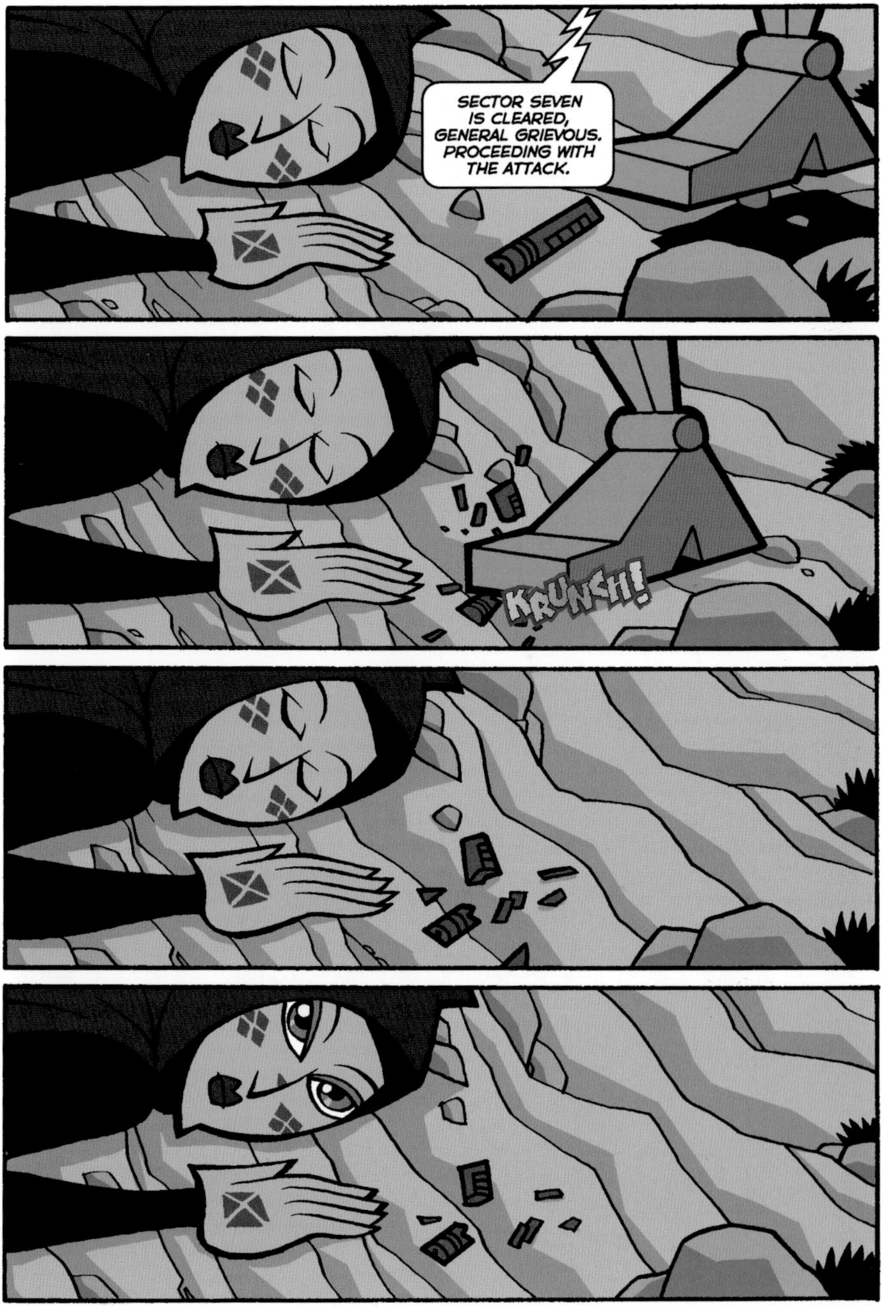
SECTOR SEVEN IS CLEARED, GENERAL GRIEVOUS. PROCEEDING WITH THE ATTACK.
KRUNCH!

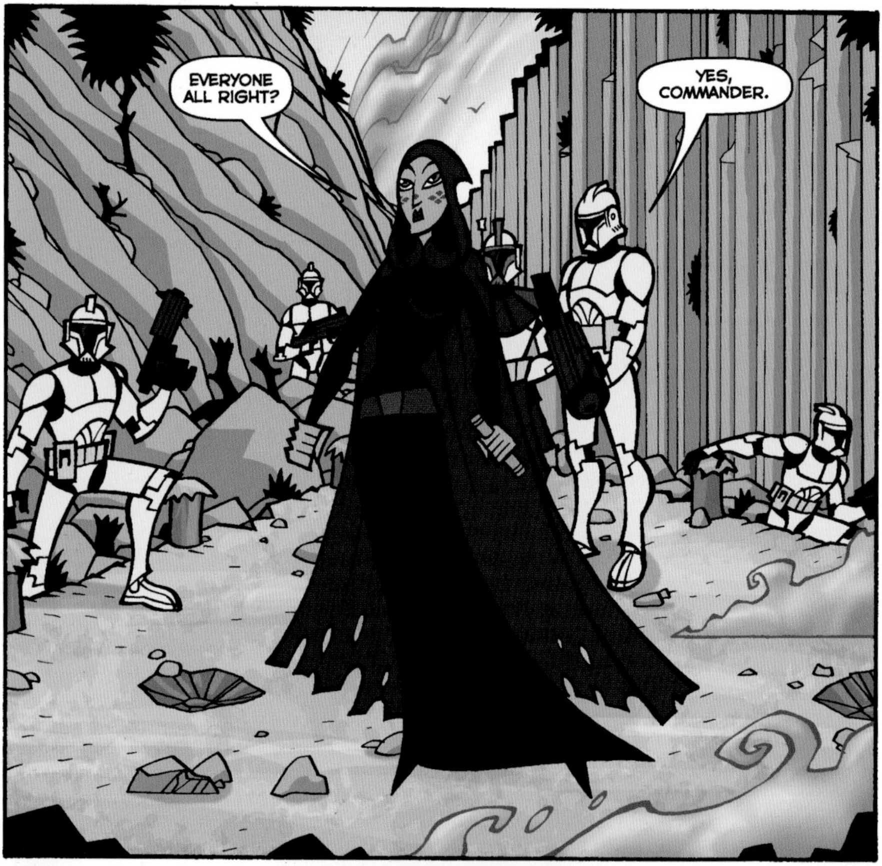
EVERYONE ALL RIGHT?
YES, COMMANDER.

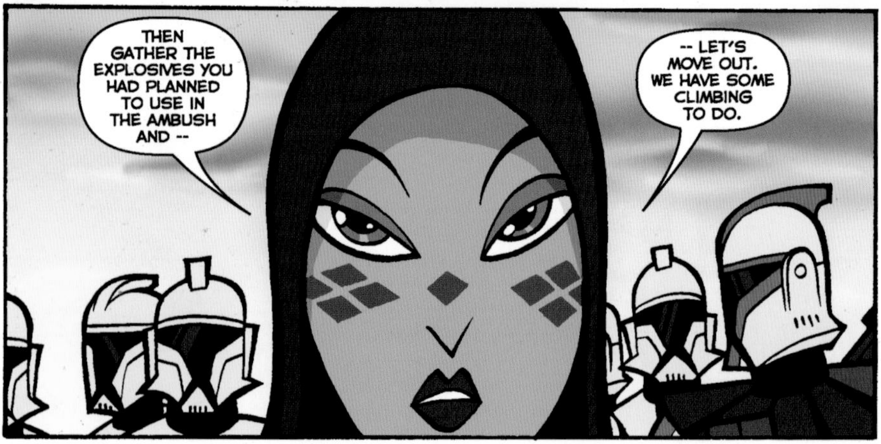
THEN GATHER THE EXPLOSIVES YOU HAD PLANNED TO USE IN THE AMBUSH AND --
-- LET'S MOVE OUT. WE HAVE SOME CLIMBING TO DO.

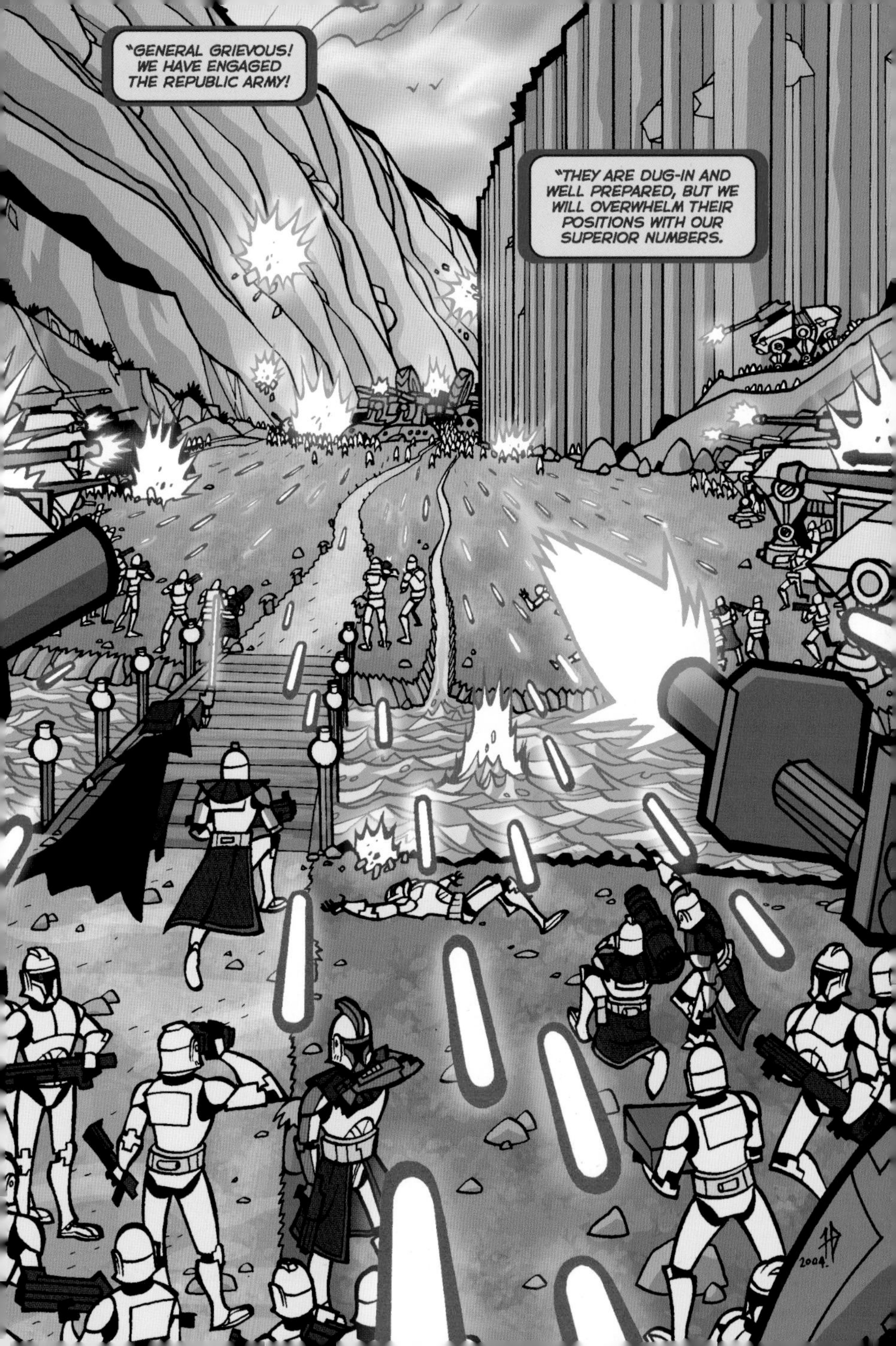
"GENERAL GRIEVOUS! WE HAVE ENGAGED THE REPUBLIC ARMY!
"THEY ARE DUG-IN AND WELL PREPARED, BUT WE WILL OVERWHELM THEIR POSITIONS WITH OUR SUPERIOR NUMBERS.

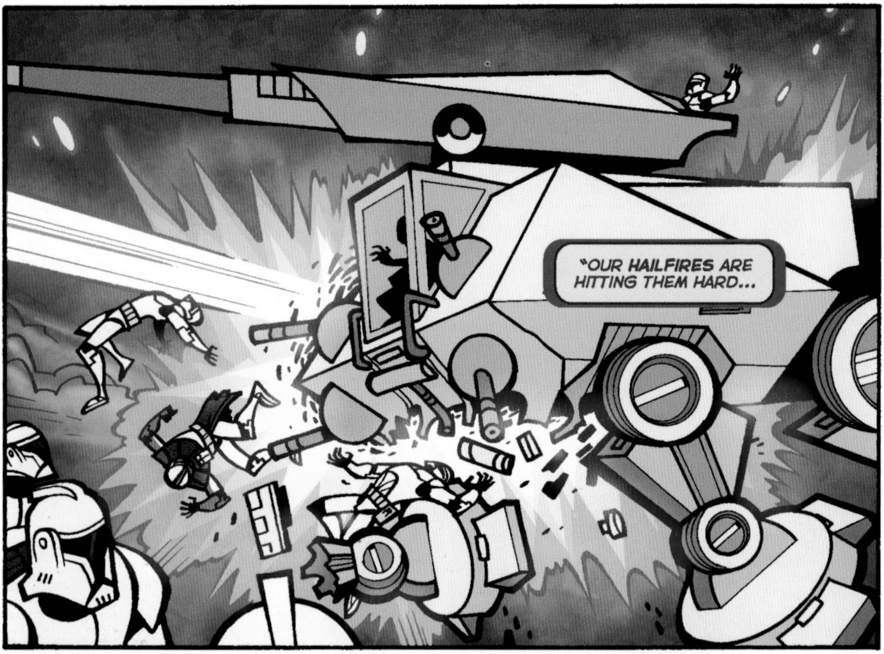
"OUR HAILFIRES ARE HITTING THEM HARD...

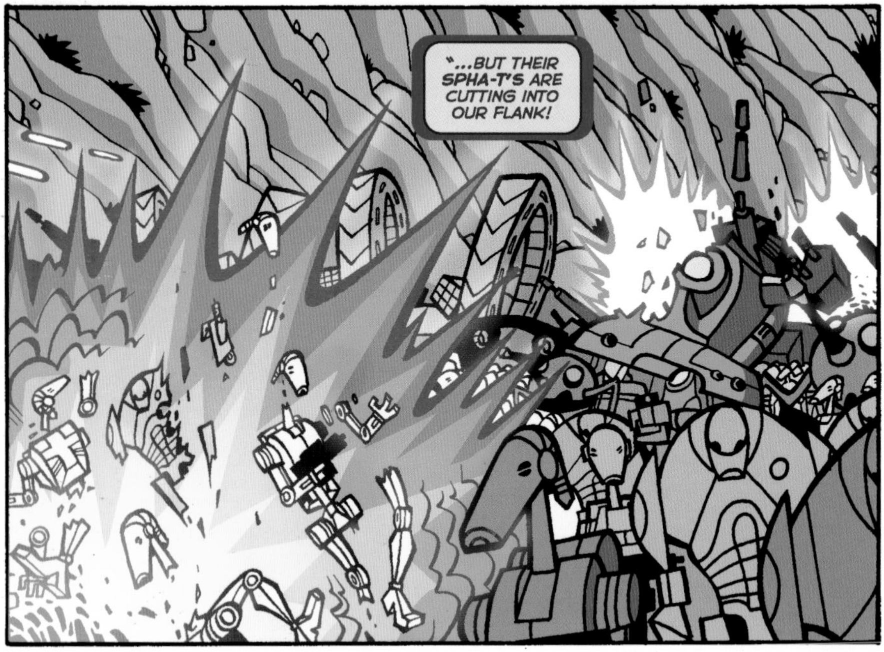
"...BUT THEIR SPHA-T'S ARE CUTTING INTO OUR FLANK!

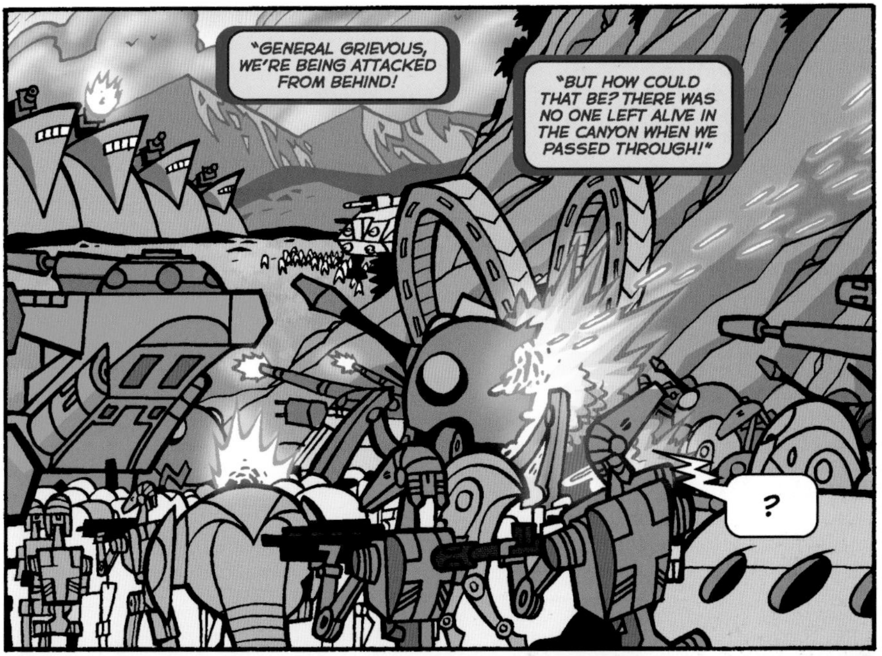
"GENERAL GRIEVOUS, WE'RE BEING ATTACKED FROM BEHIND!
"BUT HOW COULD THAT BE? THERE WAS NO ONE LEFT ALIVE IN THE CANYON WHEN WE PASSED THROUGH!"
?

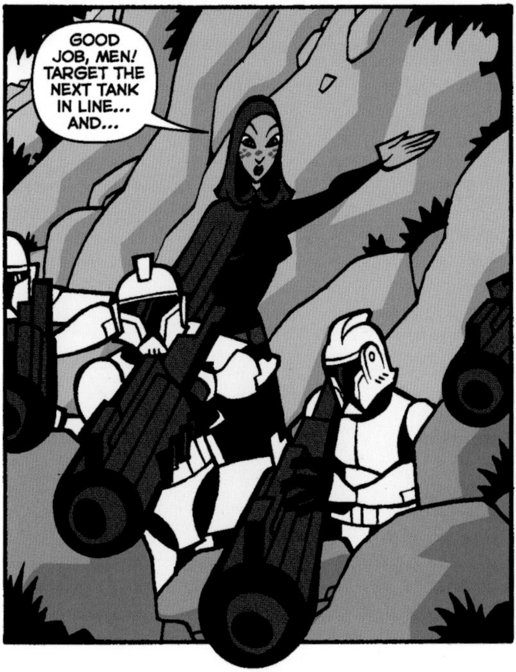
GOOD JOB, MEN! TARGET THE NEXT TANK IN LINE... AND...

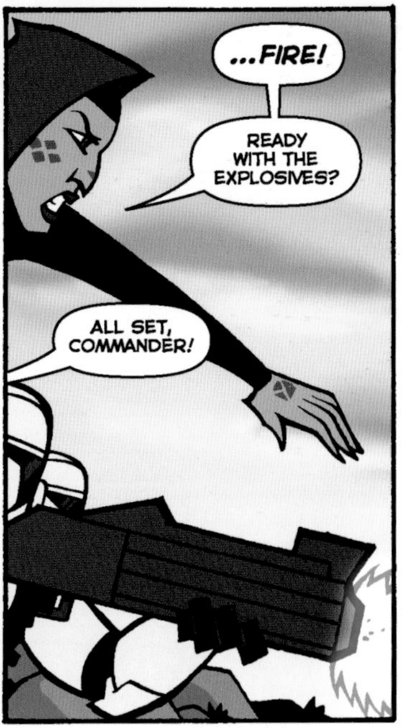
READY WITH THE EXPLOSIVES?
ALL SET, COMMANDER!
...FIRE!

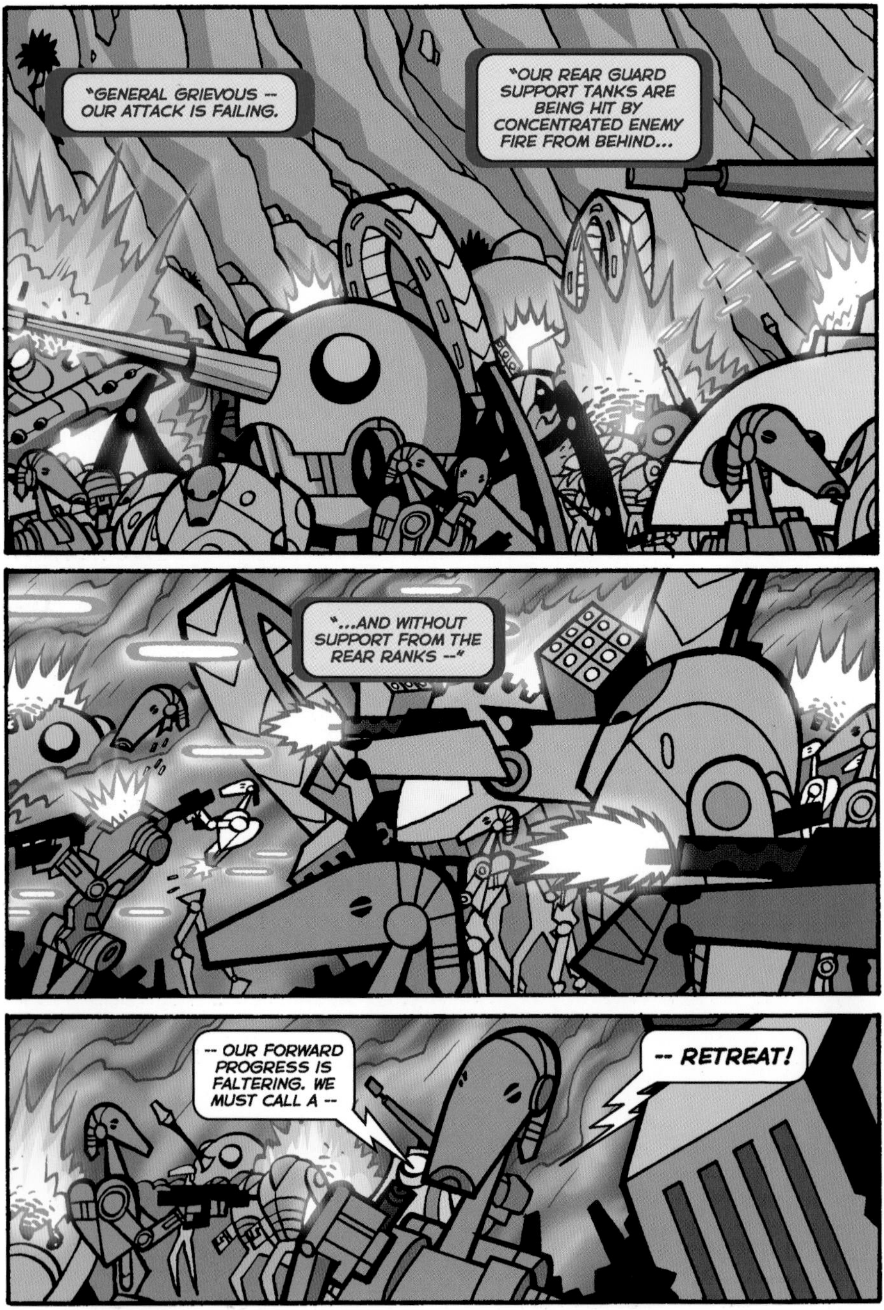
"GENERAL GRIEVOUS -- OUR ATTACK IS FAILING.
"OUR REAR GUARD SUPPORT TANKS ARE BEING HIT BY CONCENTRATED ENEMY FIRE FROM BEHIND...
"...AND WITHOUT SUPPORT FROM THE REAR RANKS --"
-- OUR FORWARD PROGRESS IS FALTERING. WE MUST CALL A --
-- RETREAT!

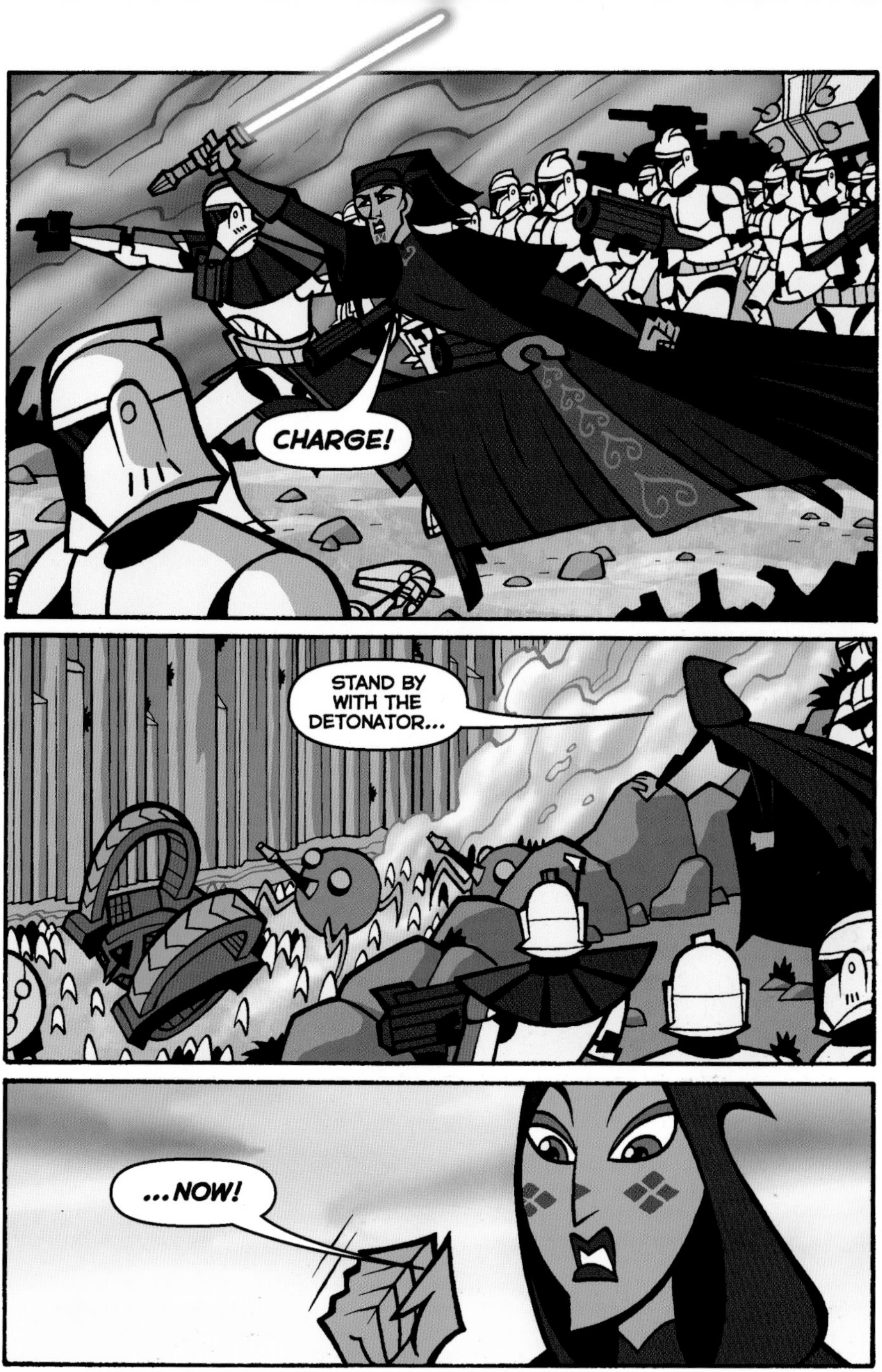
CHARGE!
STAND BY WITH THE DETONATOR...
...NOW!

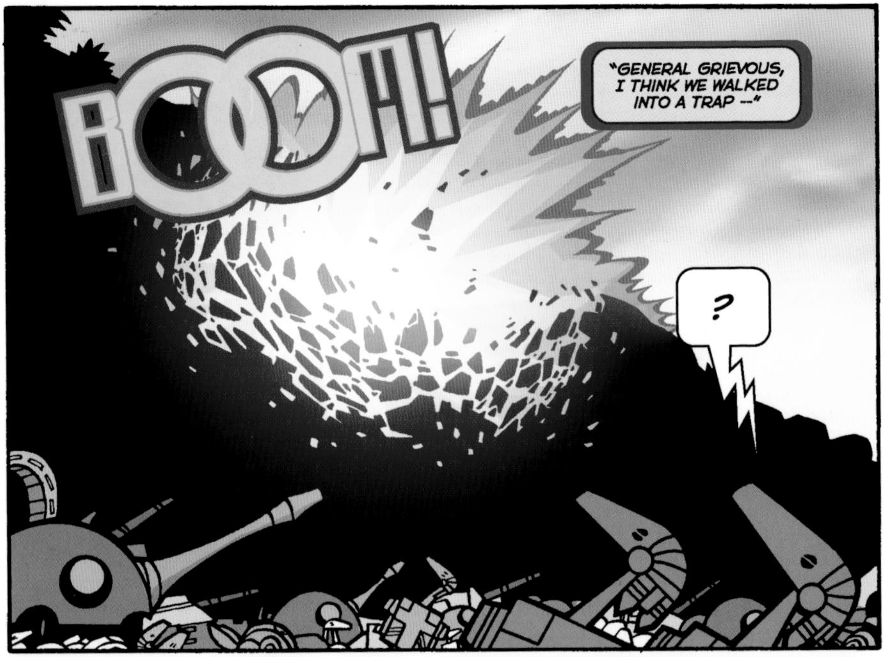
BOOM!
"GENERAL GRIEVOUS, I THINK WE WALKED INTO A TRAP --"
?

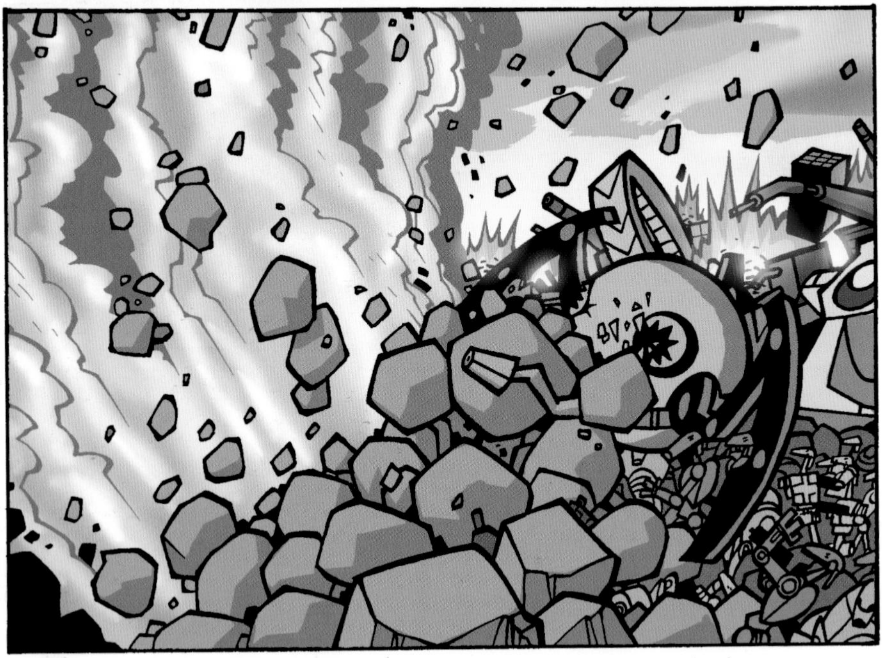

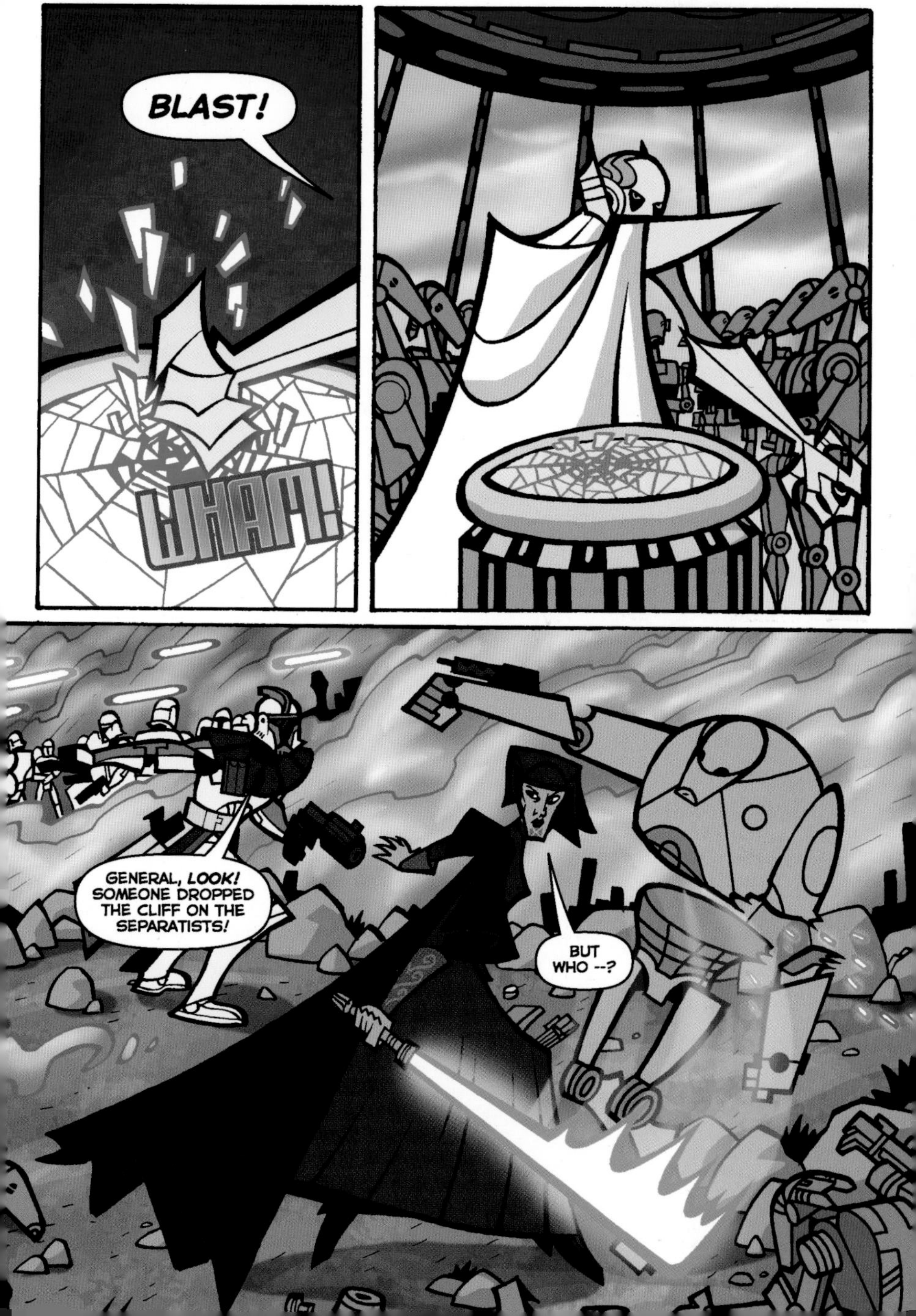
BLAST!
WHAM!
GENERAL, LOOK! SOMEONE DROPPED THE CLIFF ON THE SEPARATISTS!
BUT WHO --?

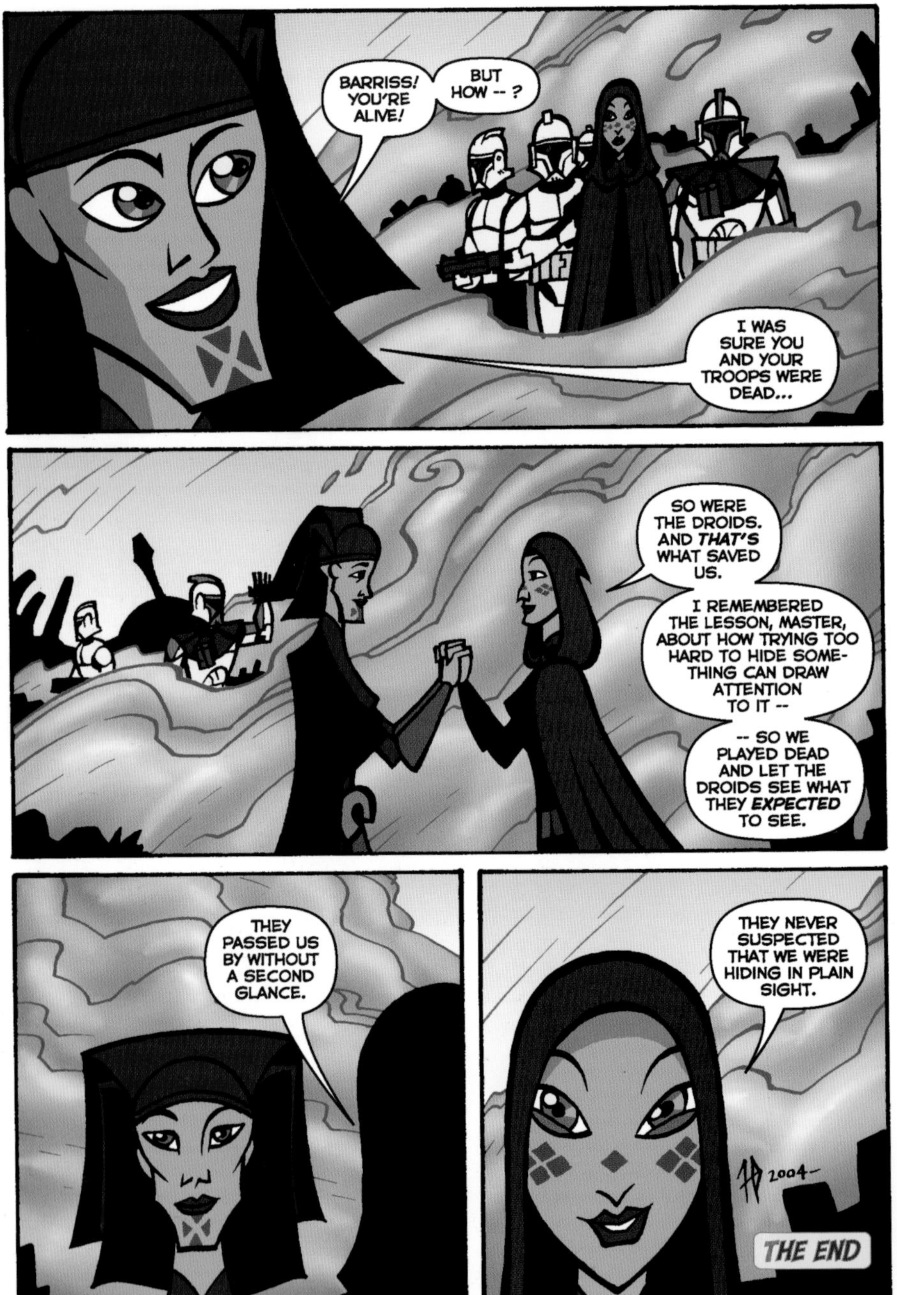
BARRISS! YOU'RE ALIVE!
BUT HOW -- ?
I WAS SURE YOU AND YOUR TROOPS WERE DEAD...
SO WERE THE DROIDS. AND *THAT'S* WHAT SAVED US.
I REMEMBERED THE LESSON, MASTER, ABOUT HOW TRYING TOO HARD TO HIDE SOME-THING CAN DRAW ATTENTION TO IT --
-- SO WE PLAYED DEAD AND LET THE DROIDS SEE WHAT THEY *EXPECTED* TO SEE.
THEY PASSED US BY WITHOUT A SECOND GLANCE.
THEY NEVER SUSPECTED THAT WE WERE HIDING IN PLAIN SIGHT.
2004
THE END

GENTLE GIANT STUDIOS, DARK HORSE COMICS, AND LUCASFILM LTD. PRESENT

LUKE SKYWALKER™ X-WING™ PILOT

6 1/4" TALL,
FULLY PAINTED
ITEM #10-243
$45.00

GAMORREAN GUARD™

5 1/2" TALL,
FULLY PAINTED
ITEM #11-946
$45.00

BOSSK™

6" TALL,
FULLY PAINTED
ITEM 10-165
$45.00

DELUXE STORMTROOPER™

6" TALL,
FULLY PAINTED,
POSABLE BUST
ITEM #10-238
$50.00

MINI-BUSTS
CONTINUING A NEW ERA IN *STAR WARS* COLLECTIBLES

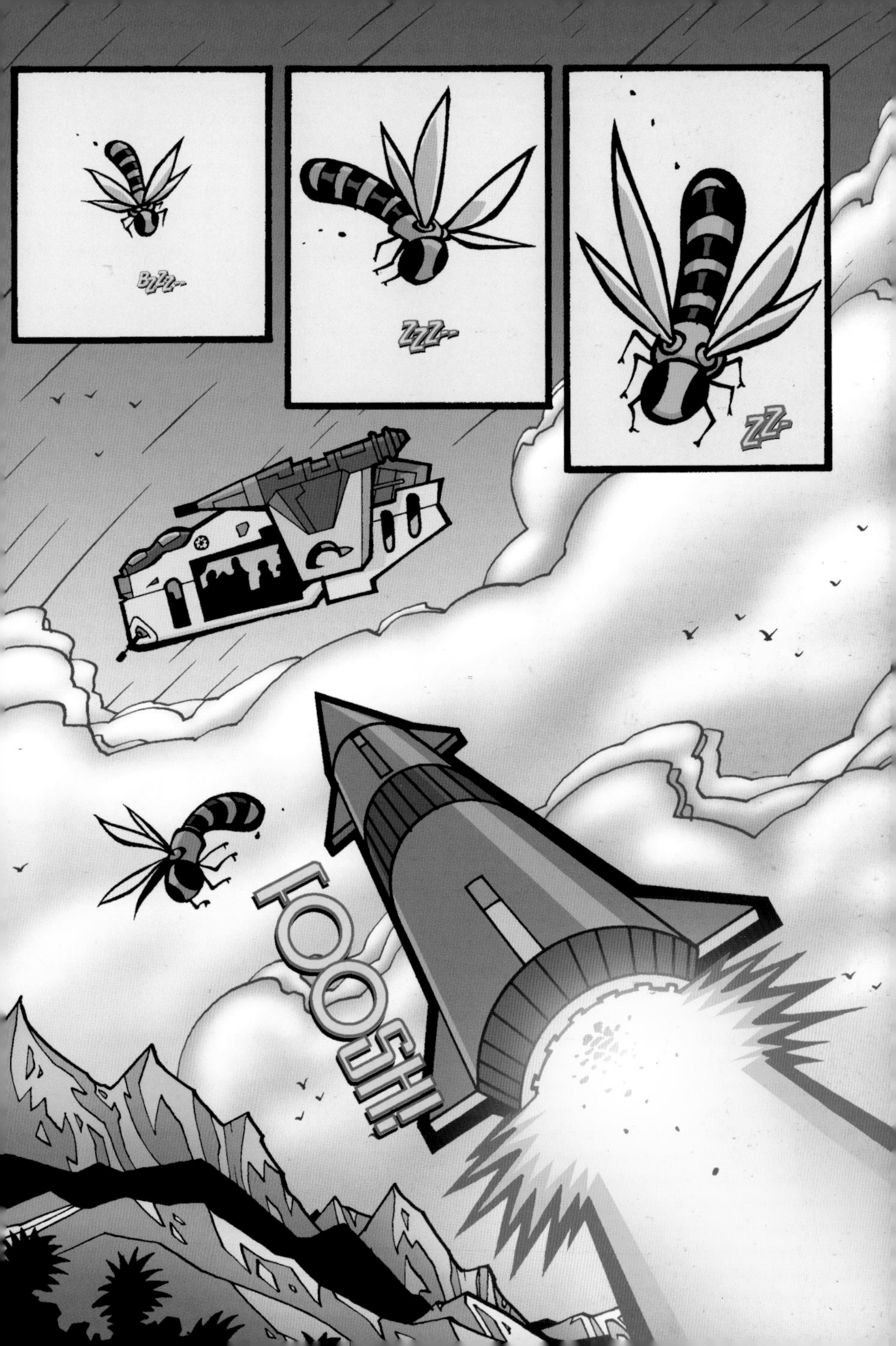
BZZZ--
ZZZ--
ZZ-
FOOSH!

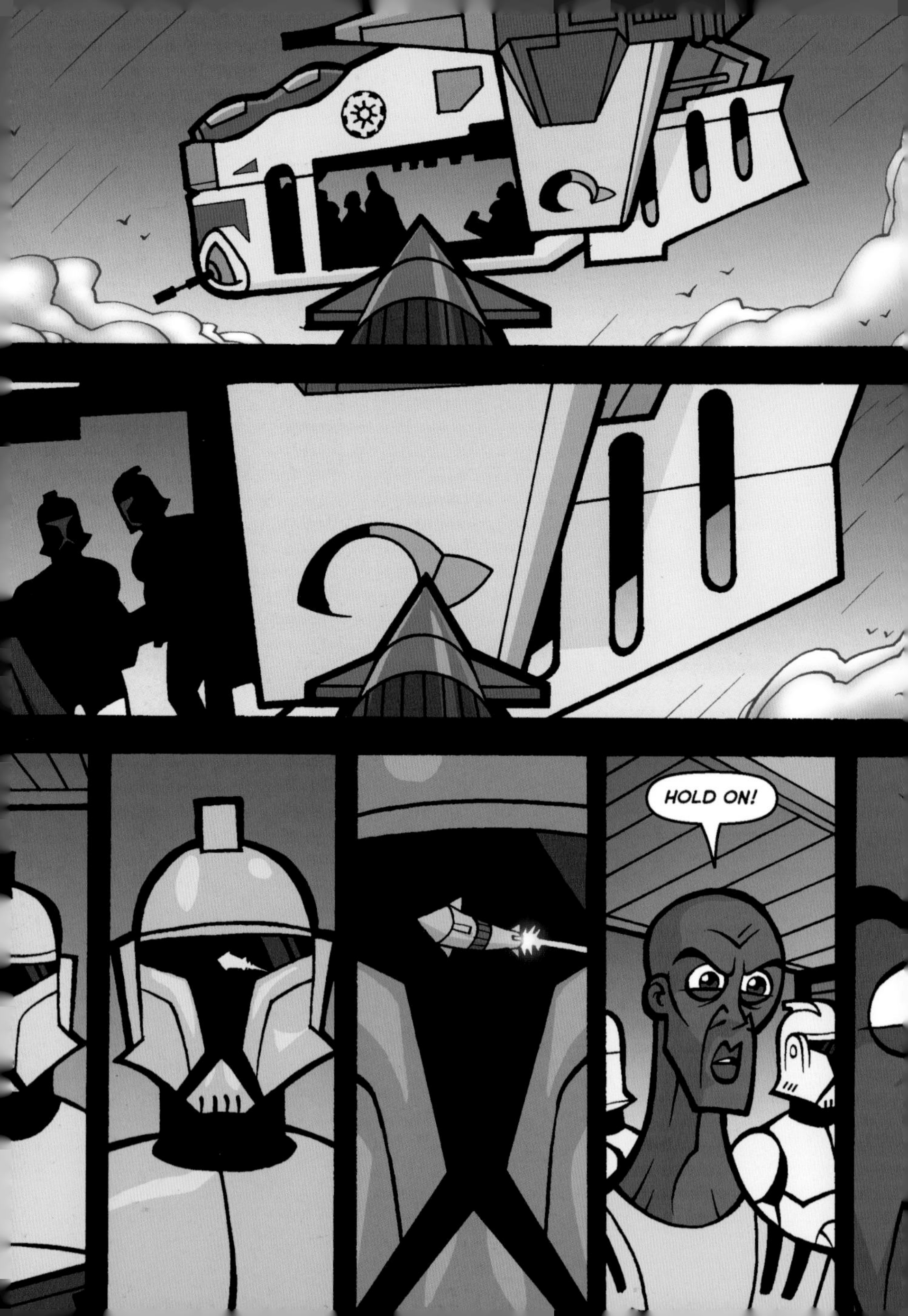
HOLD ON!

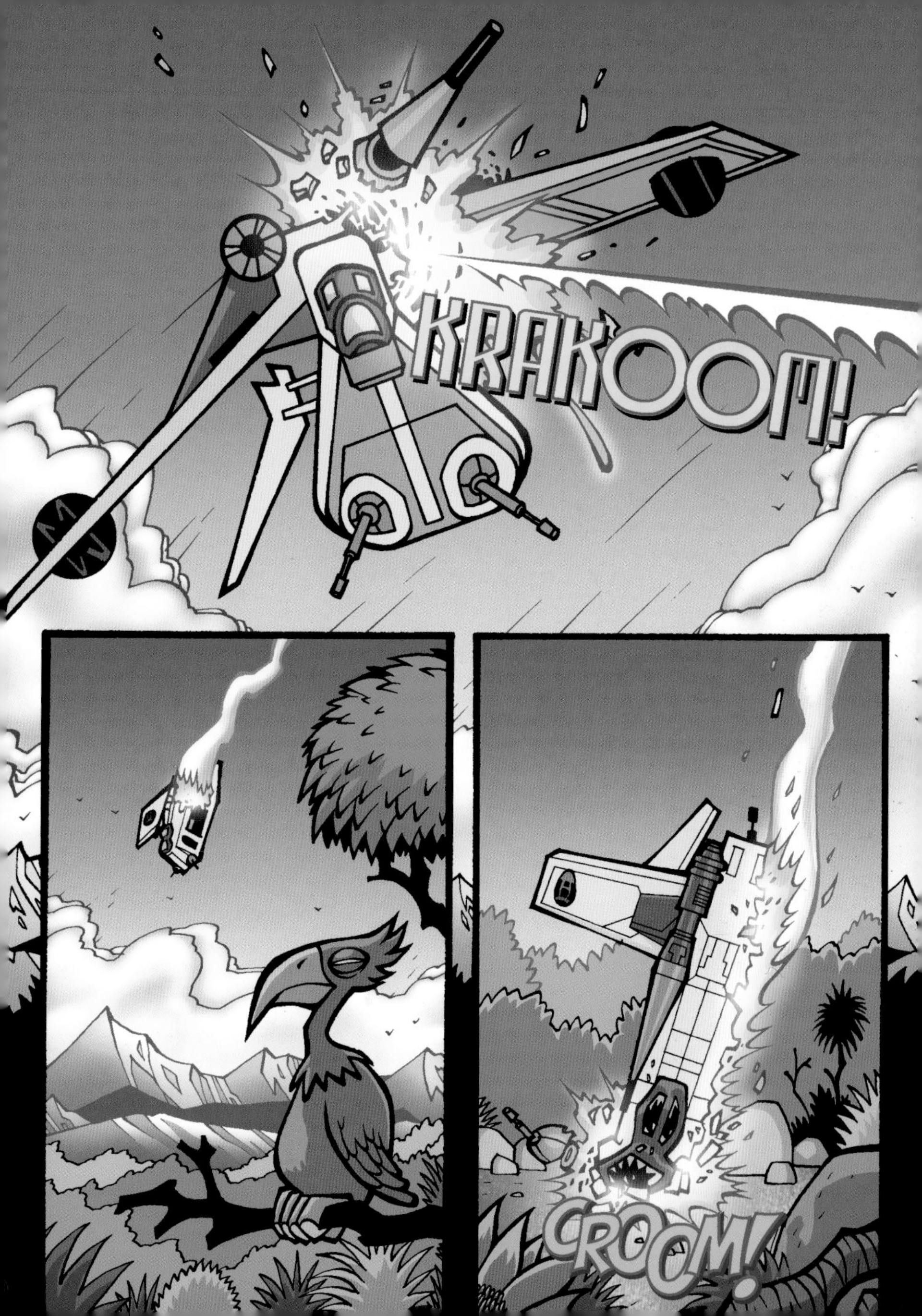
KRAKOOM!
CROOM!

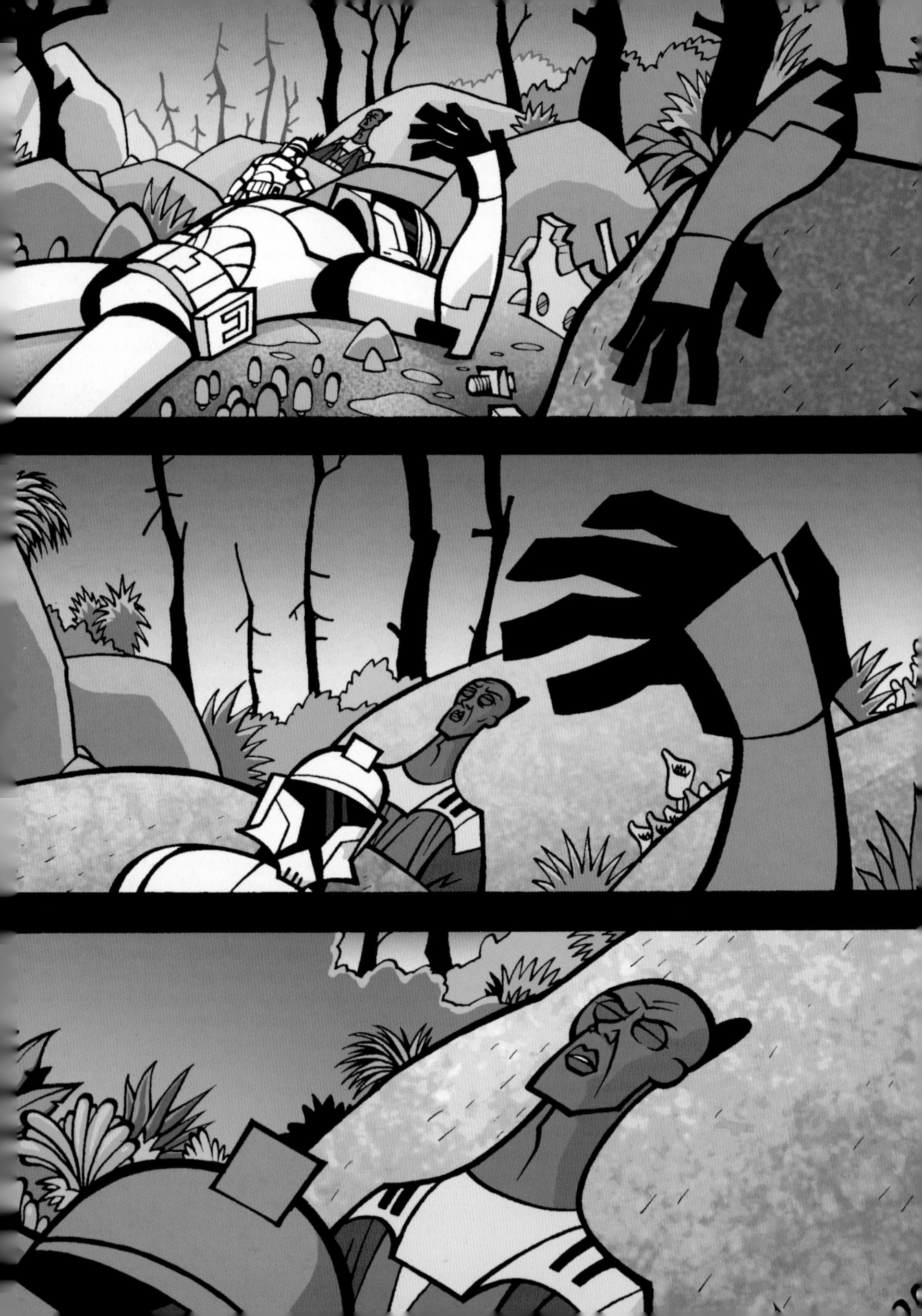

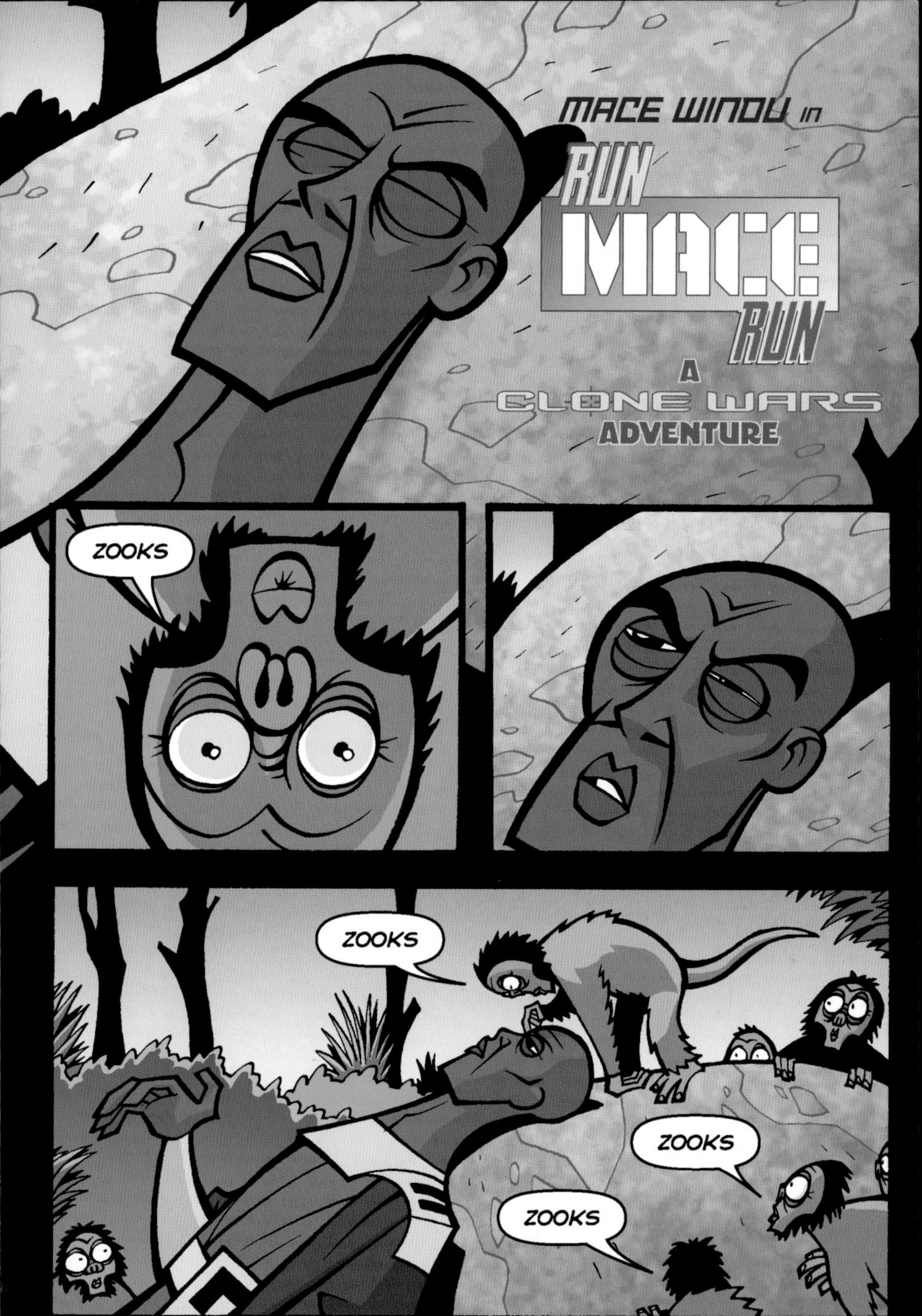
MACE WINDU in
RUN MACE RUN
A CLONE WARS ADVENTURE
ZOOKS
ZOOKS
ZOOKS
ZOOKS

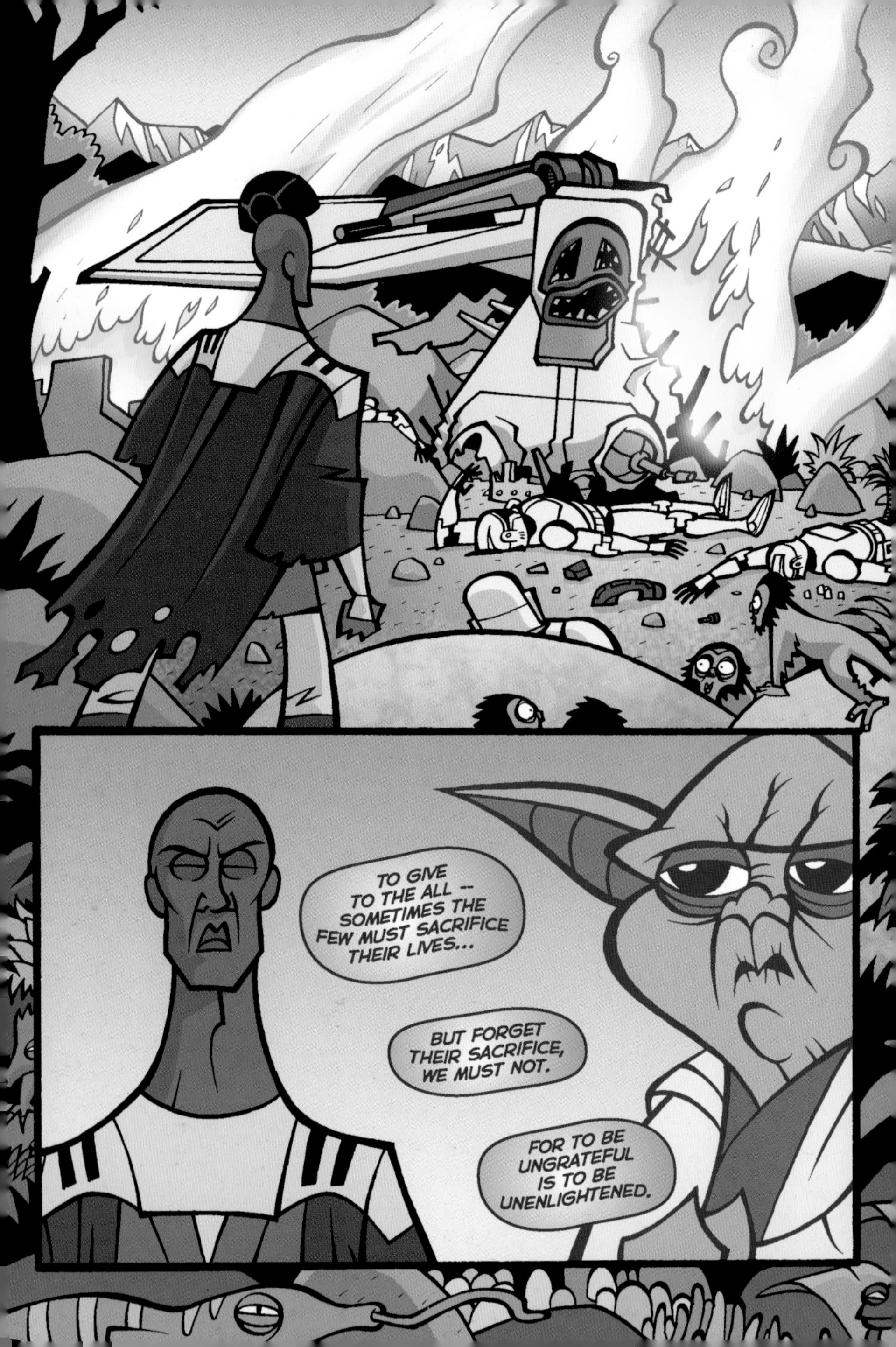
TO GIVE TO THE ALL -- SOMETIMES THE FEW MUST SACRIFICE THEIR LIVES...
BUT FORGET THEIR SACRIFICE, WE MUST NOT.
FOR TO BE UNGRATEFUL IS TO BE UNENLIGHTENED.

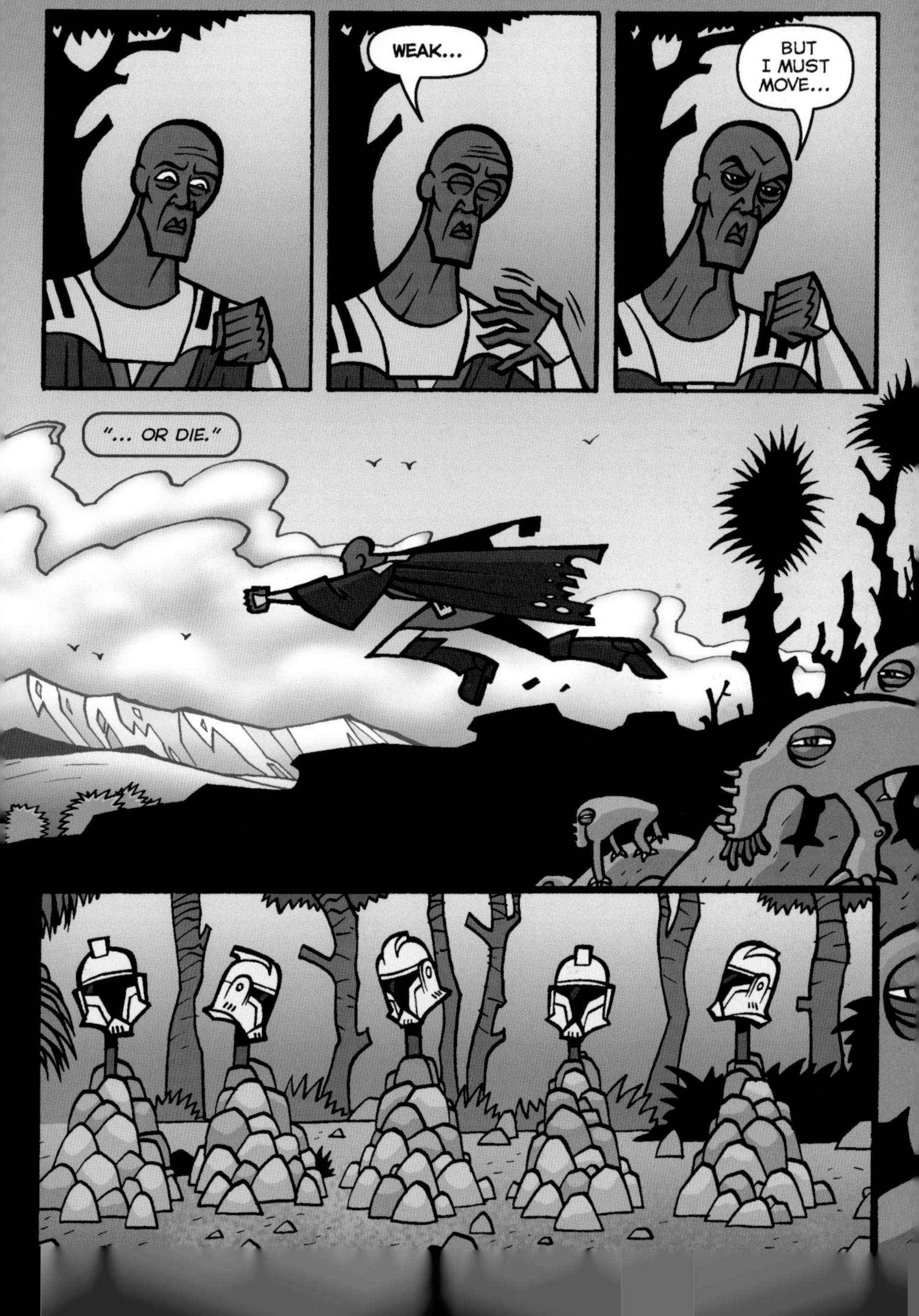
WEAK...
BUT I MUST MOVE...
"... OR DIE."

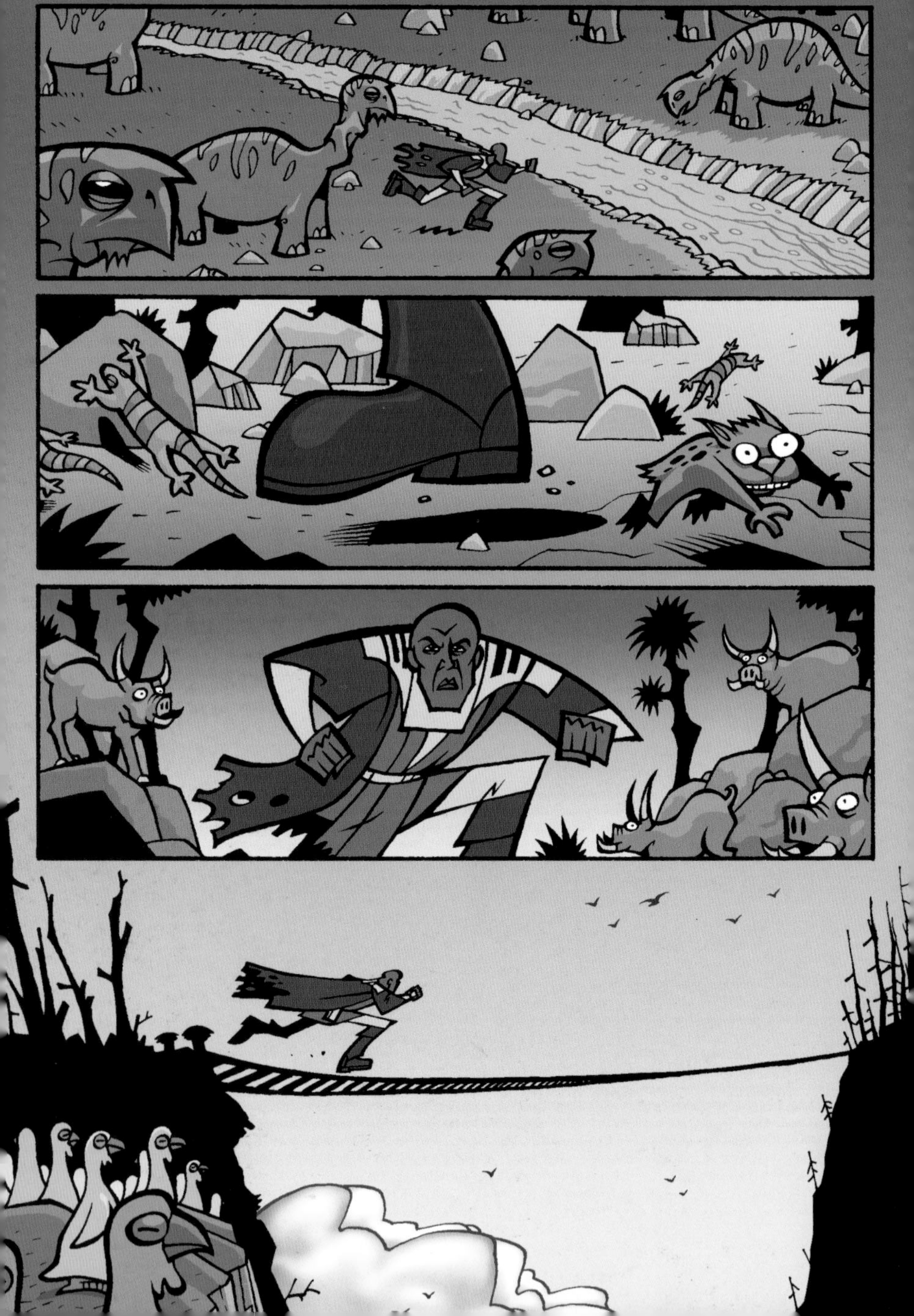

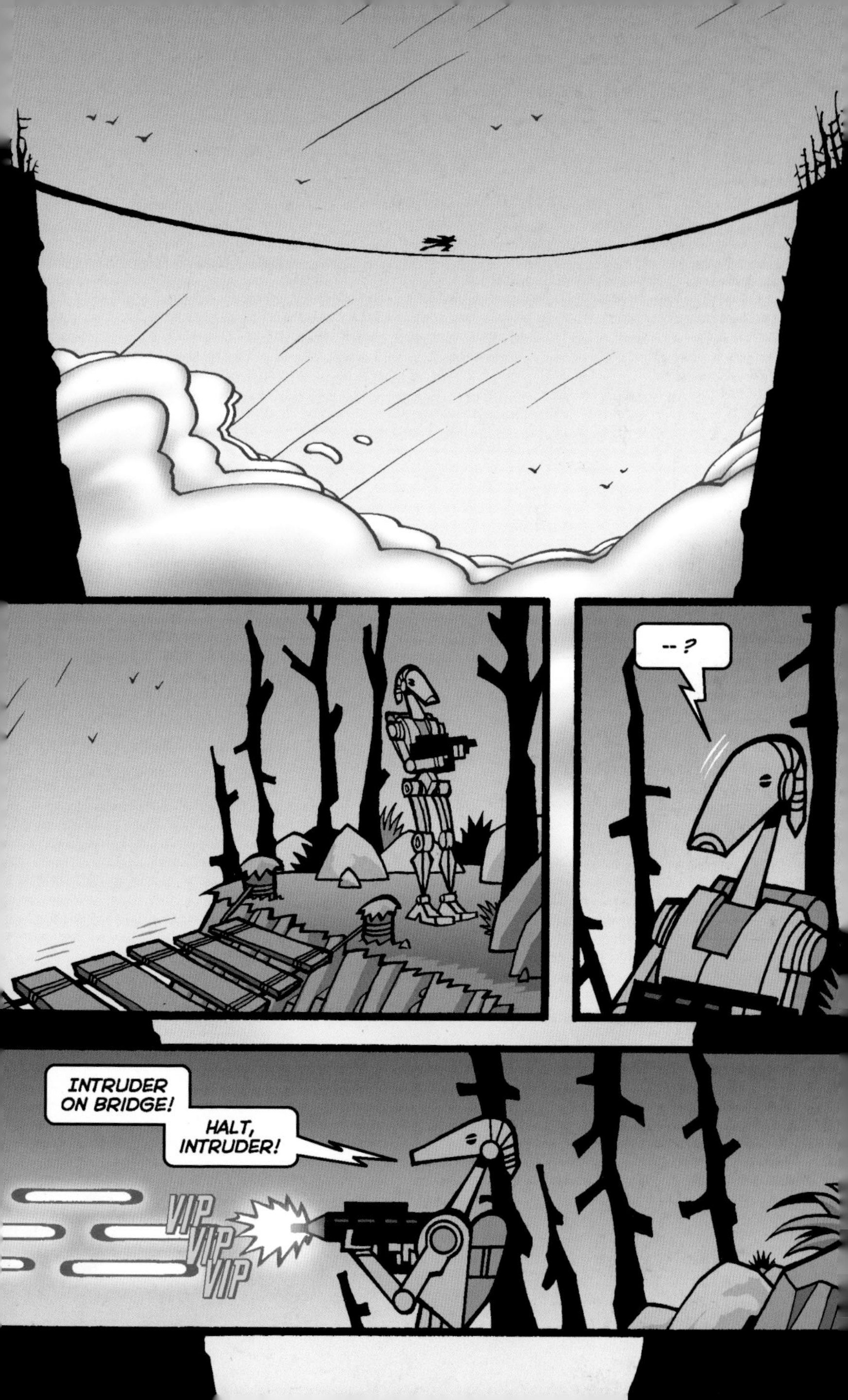
-- ?
INTRUDER ON BRIDGE!
HALT, INTRUDER!
VIP VIP VIP

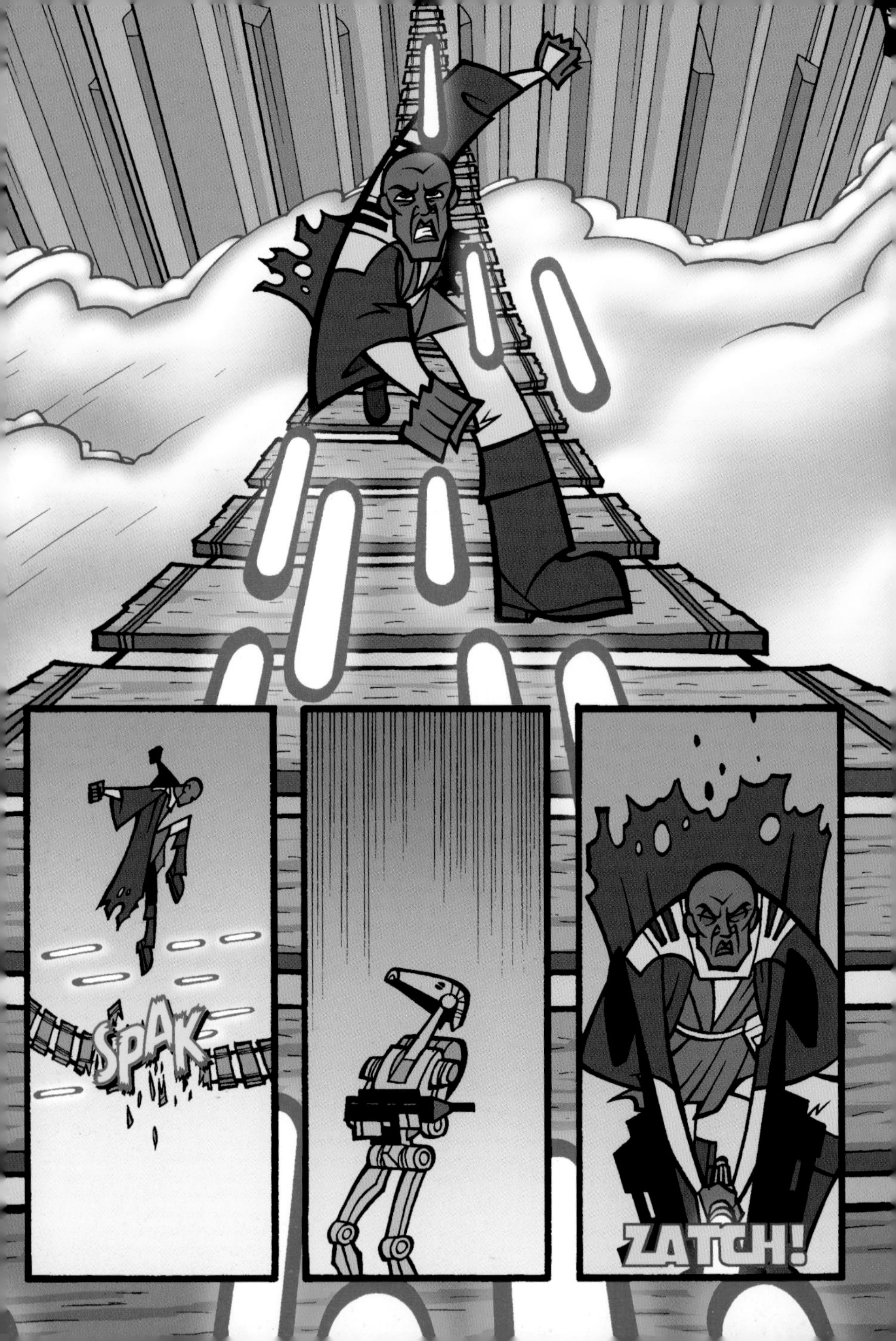
SPAK
ZATCH!

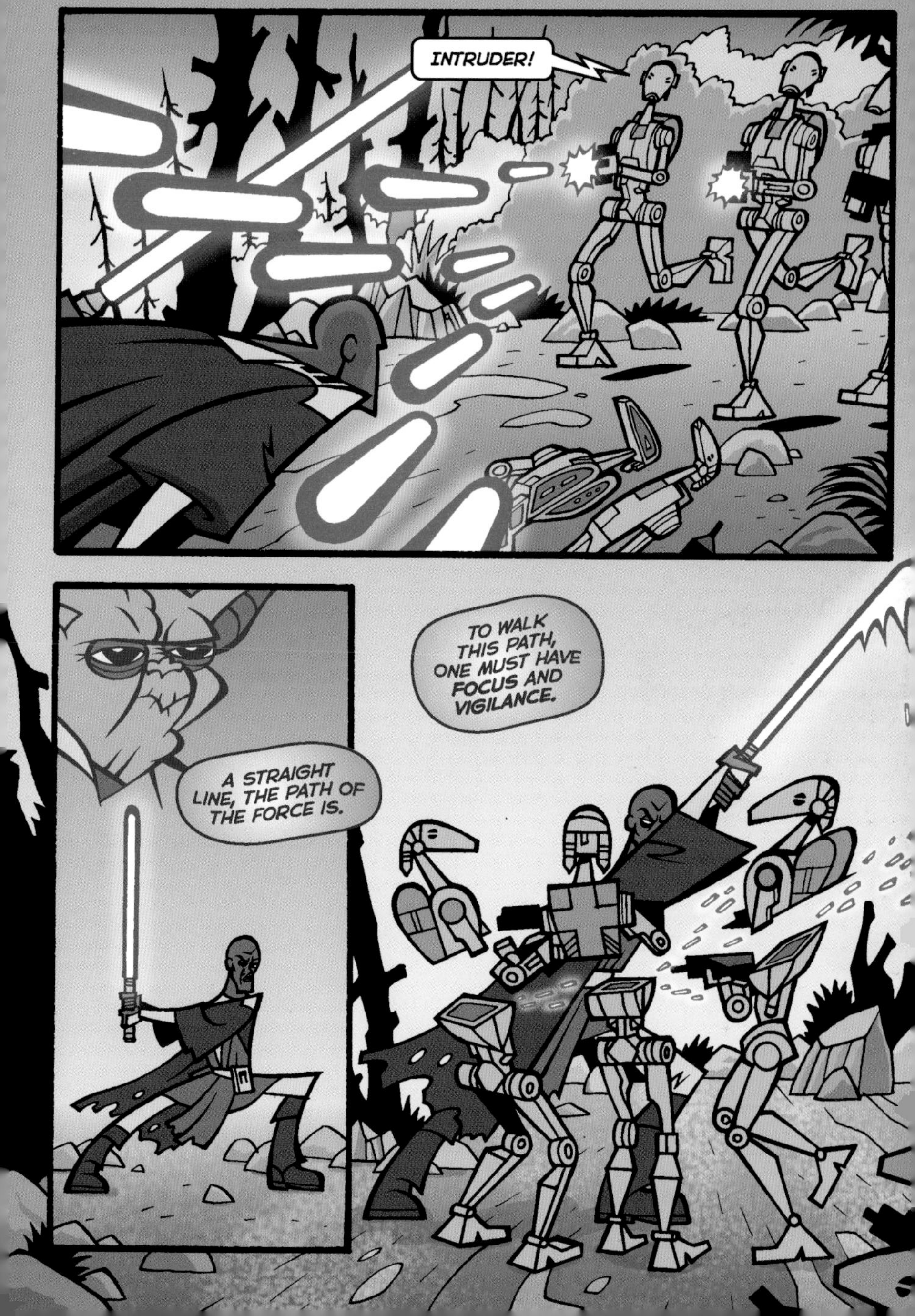
INTRUDER!
A STRAIGHT LINE, THE PATH OF THE FORCE IS.
TO WALK THIS PATH, ONE MUST HAVE FOCUS AND VIGILANCE.

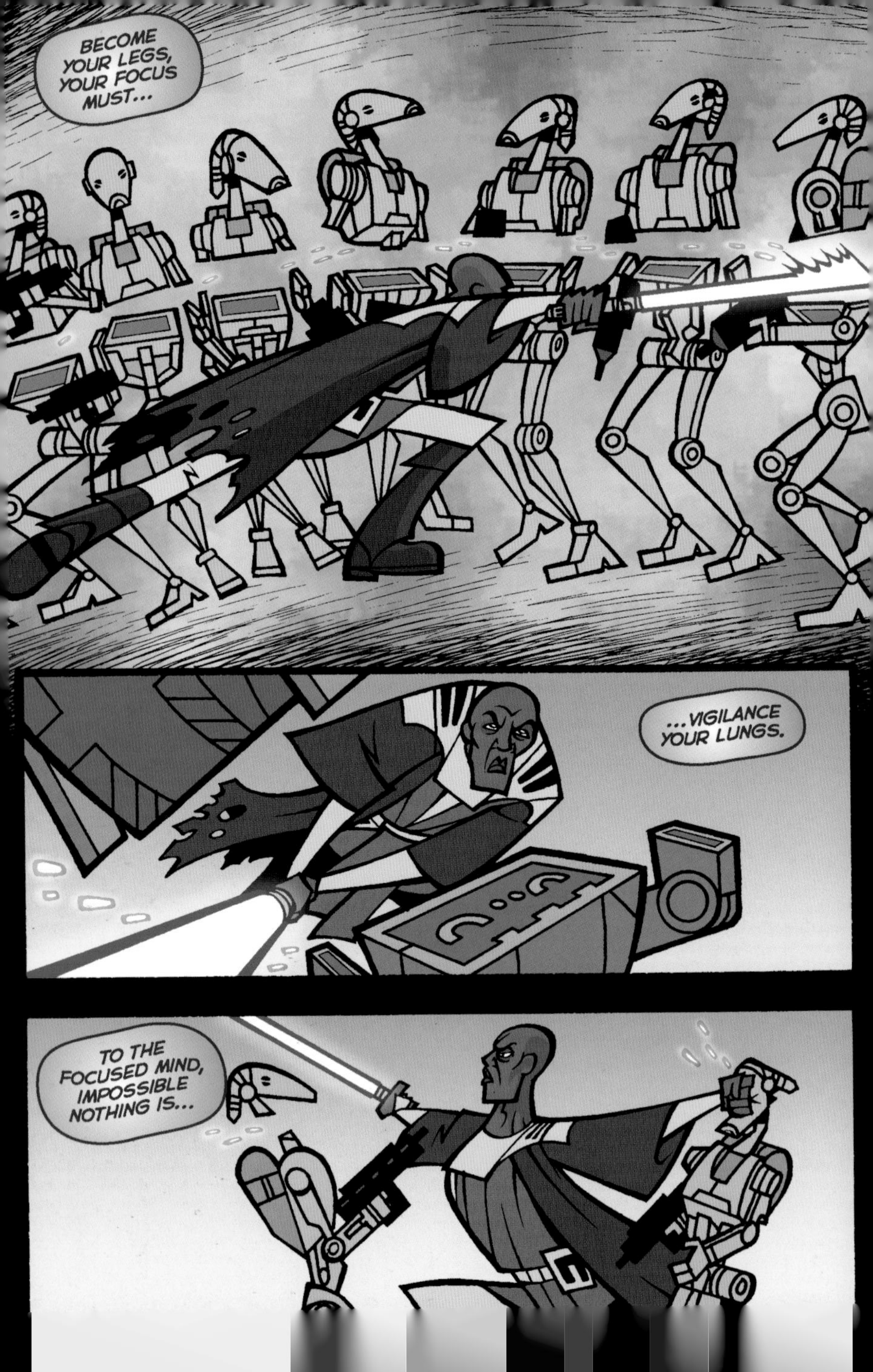
BECOME YOUR LEGS, YOUR FOCUS MUST...
...VIGILANCE YOUR LUNGS.
TO THE FOCUSED MIND, IMPOSSIBLE NOTHING IS...

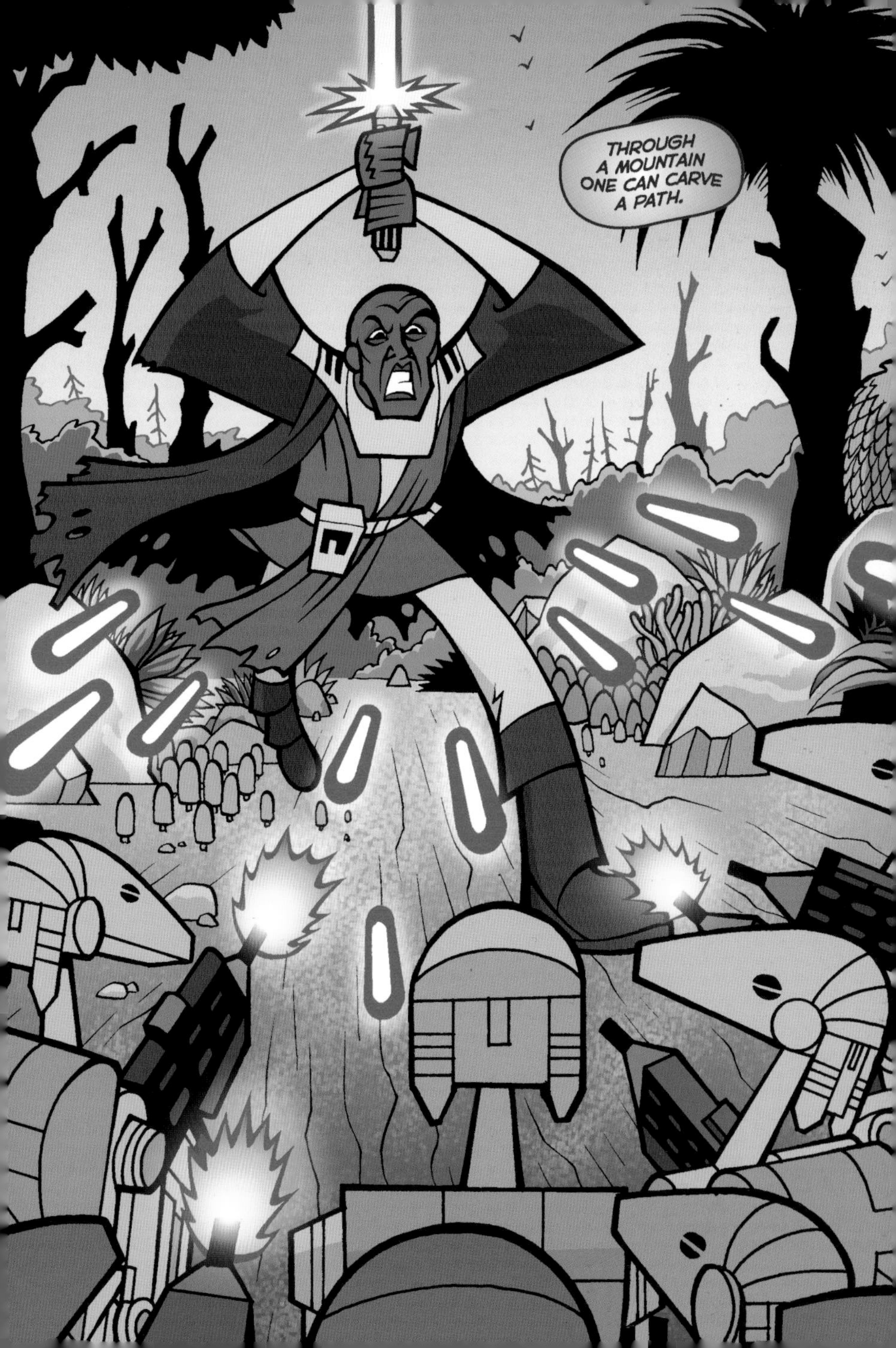
THROUGH A MOUNTAIN ONE CAN CARVE A PATH.

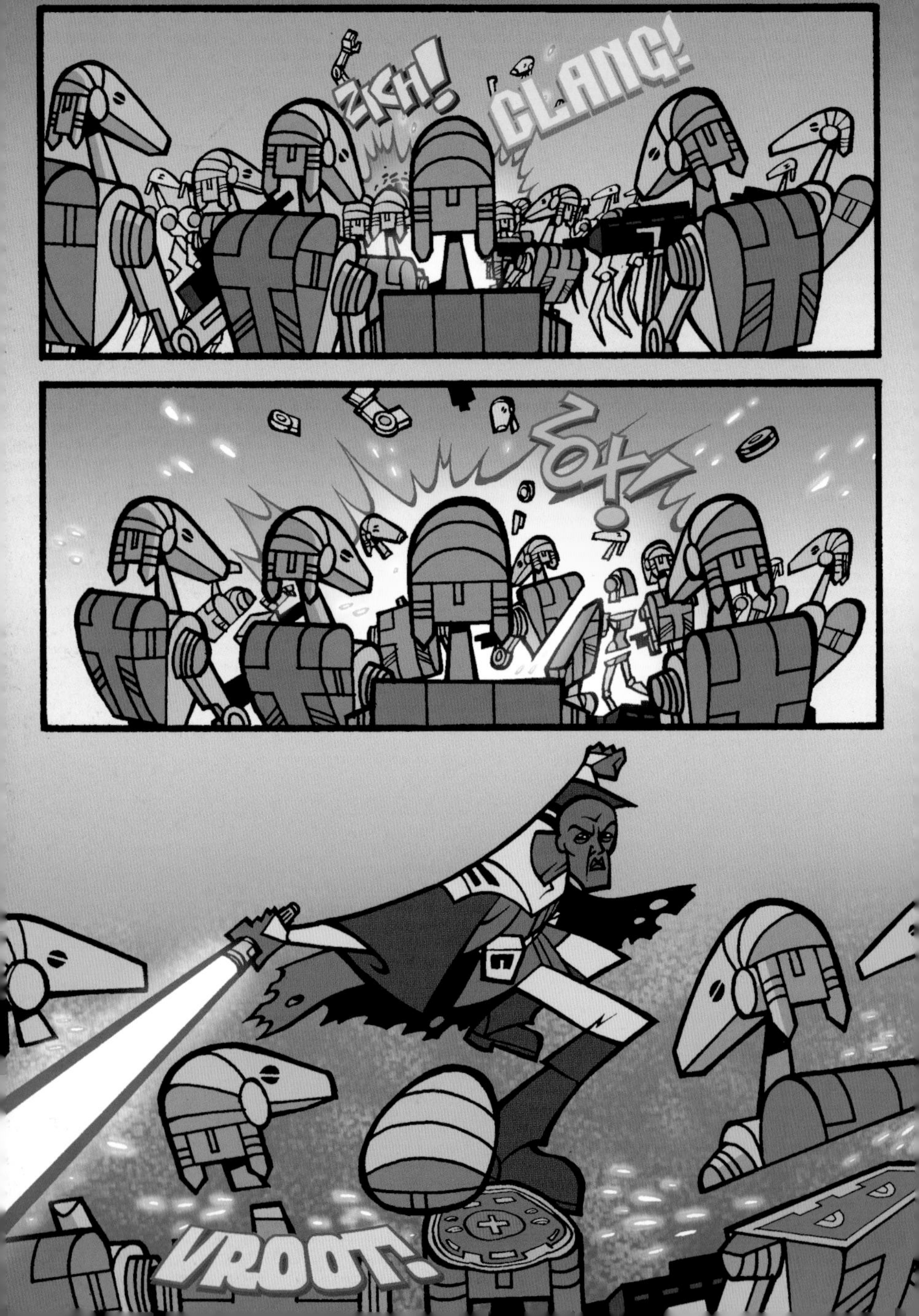
ZICH!
CLANG!
ZOT!
VROOT!

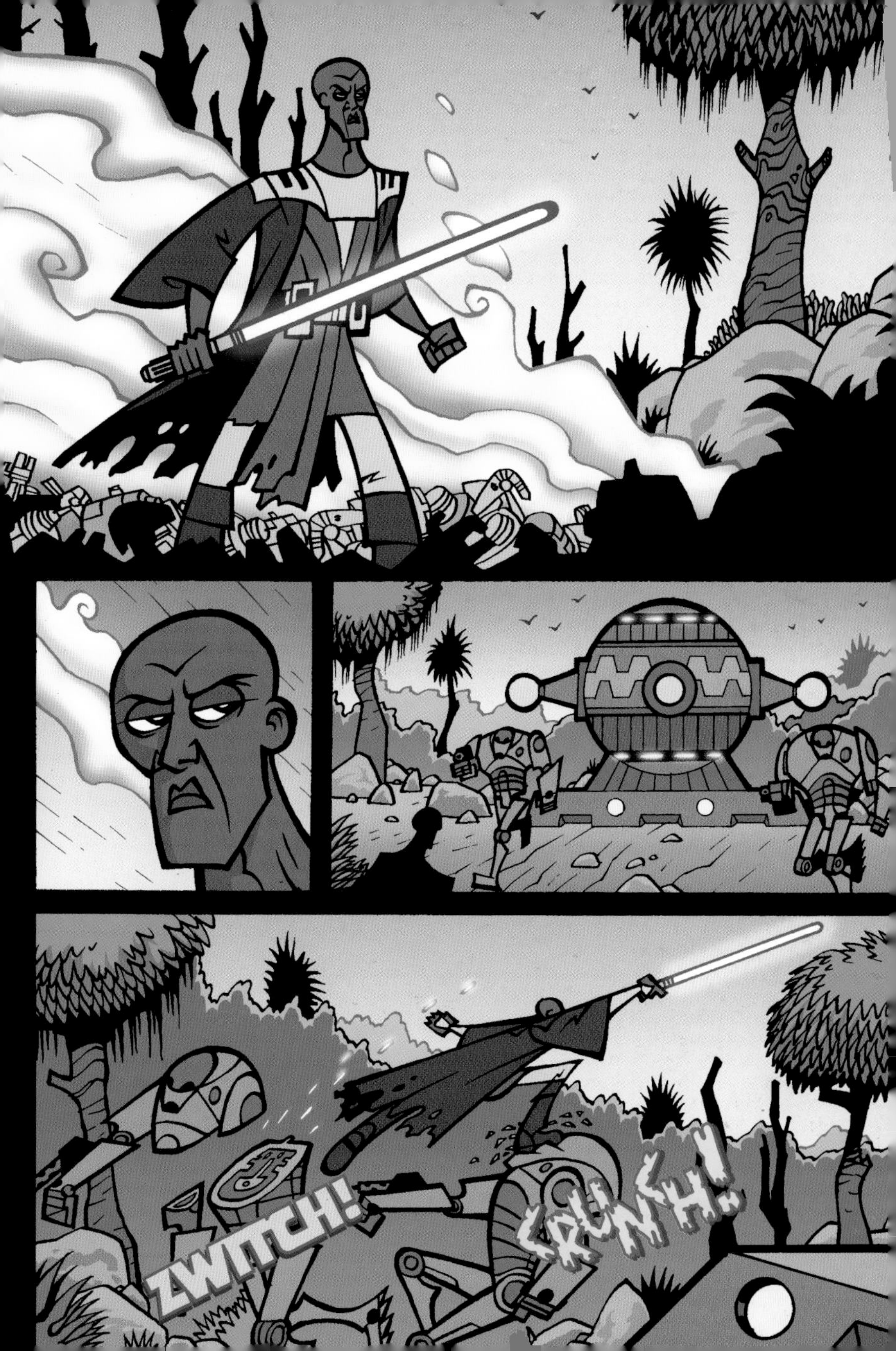
ZWITCH!
CRUNCH!

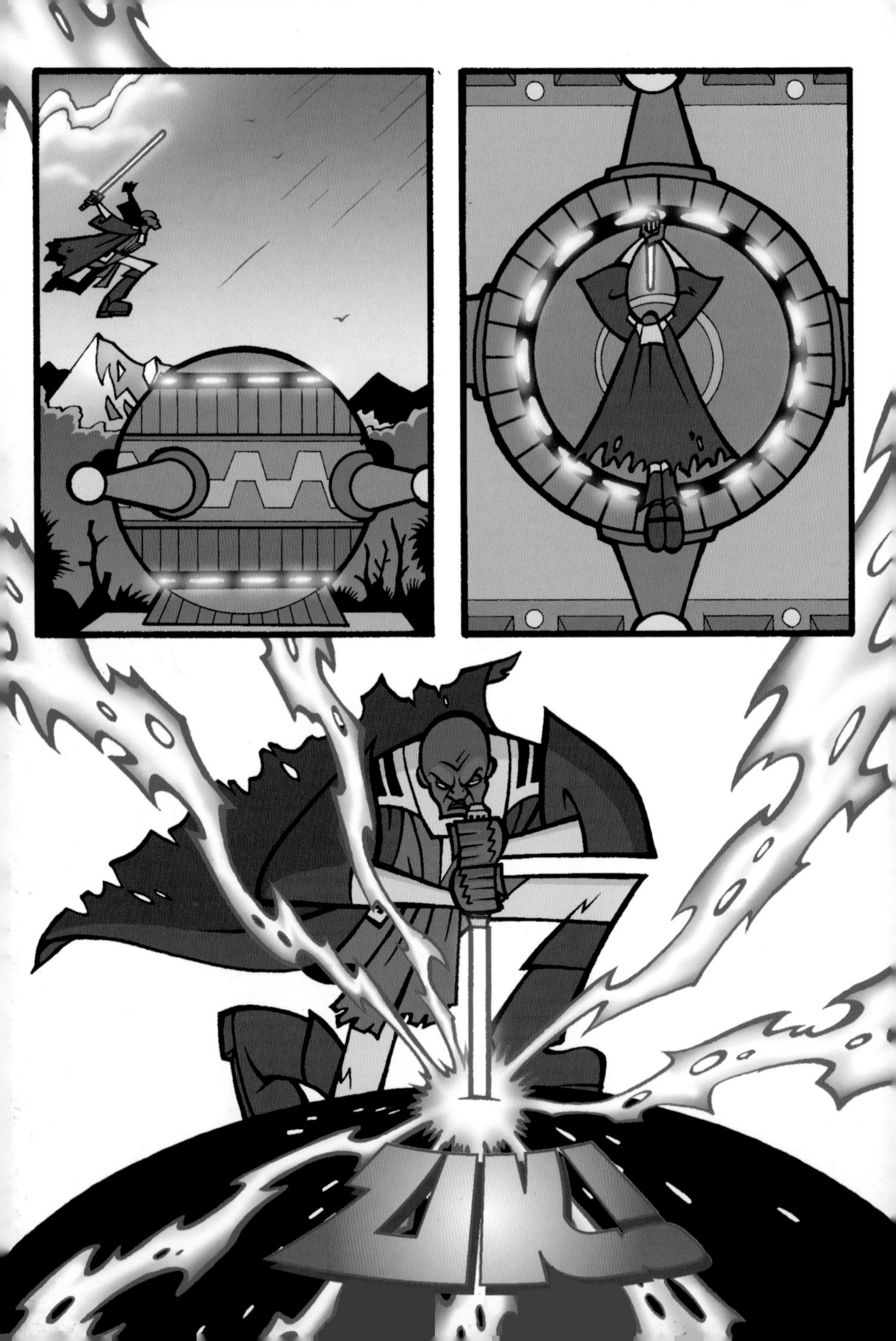

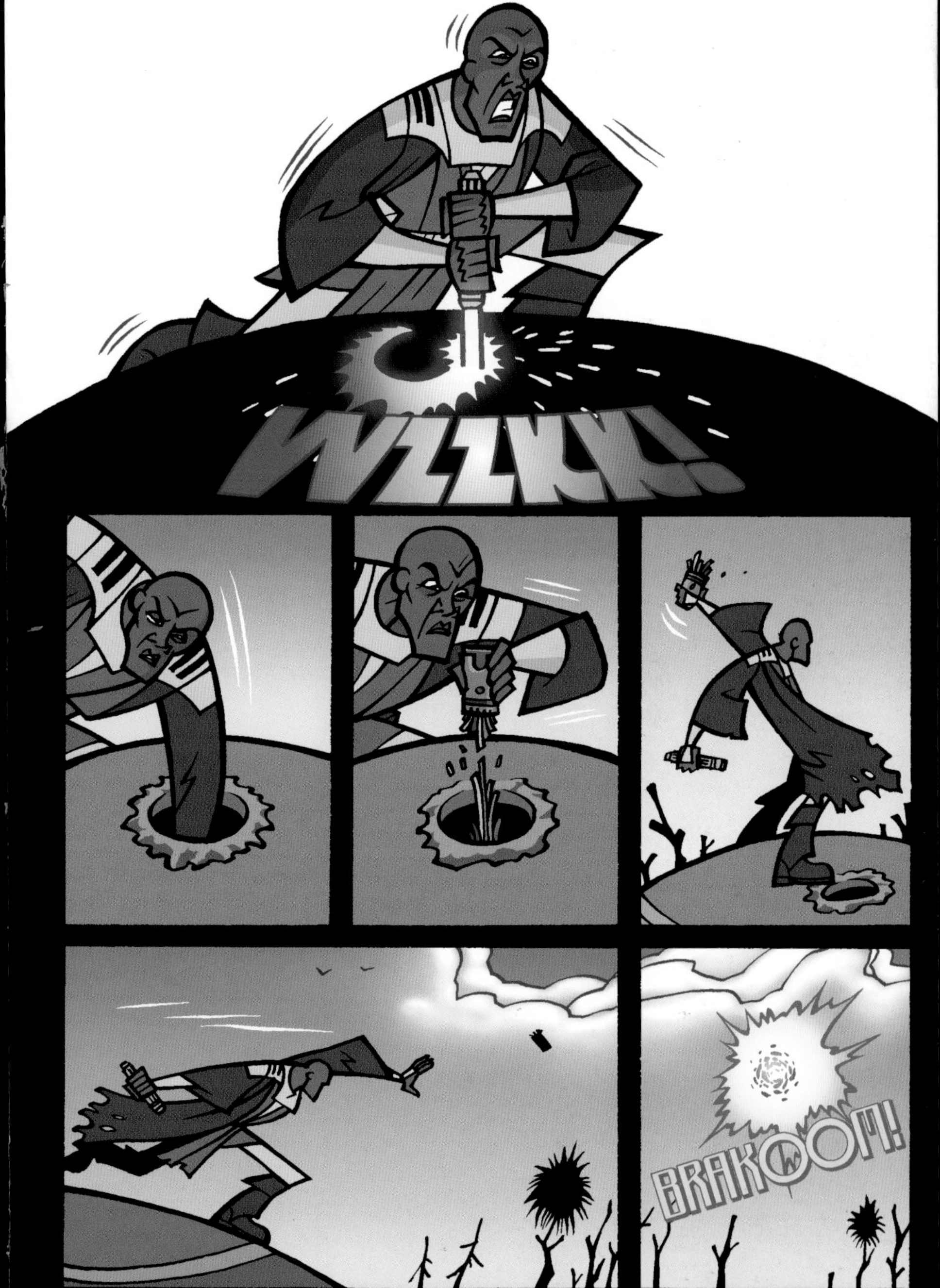
VVZZKKK!!
BRAKOOM!

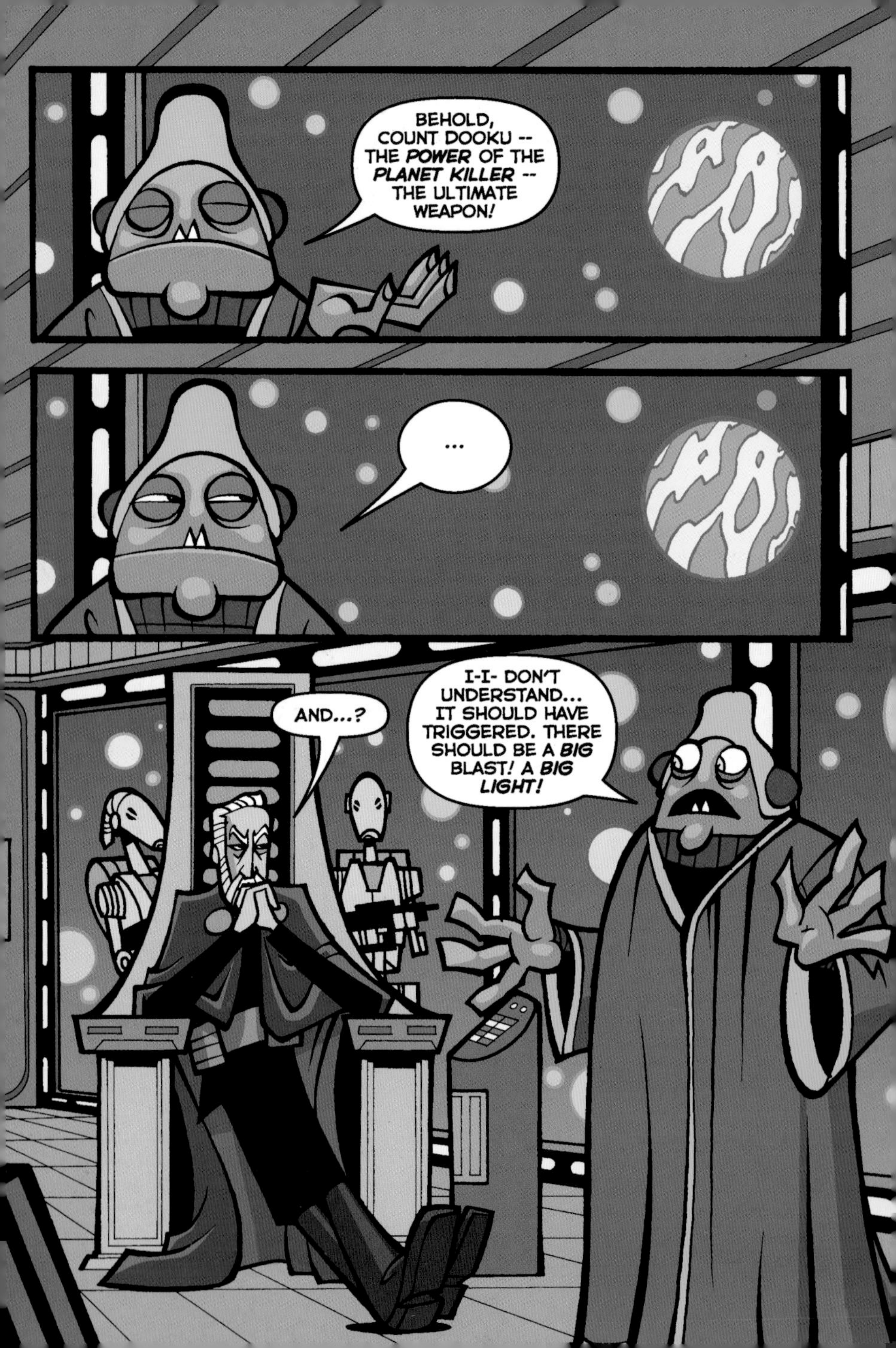
BEHOLD, COUNT DOOKU -- THE *POWER* OF THE *PLANET KILLER* -- THE ULTIMATE WEAPON!
...
AND...?
I-I- DON'T UNDERSTAND... IT SHOULD HAVE TRIGGERED. THERE SHOULD BE A *BIG* BLAST! A *BIG* *LIGHT!*

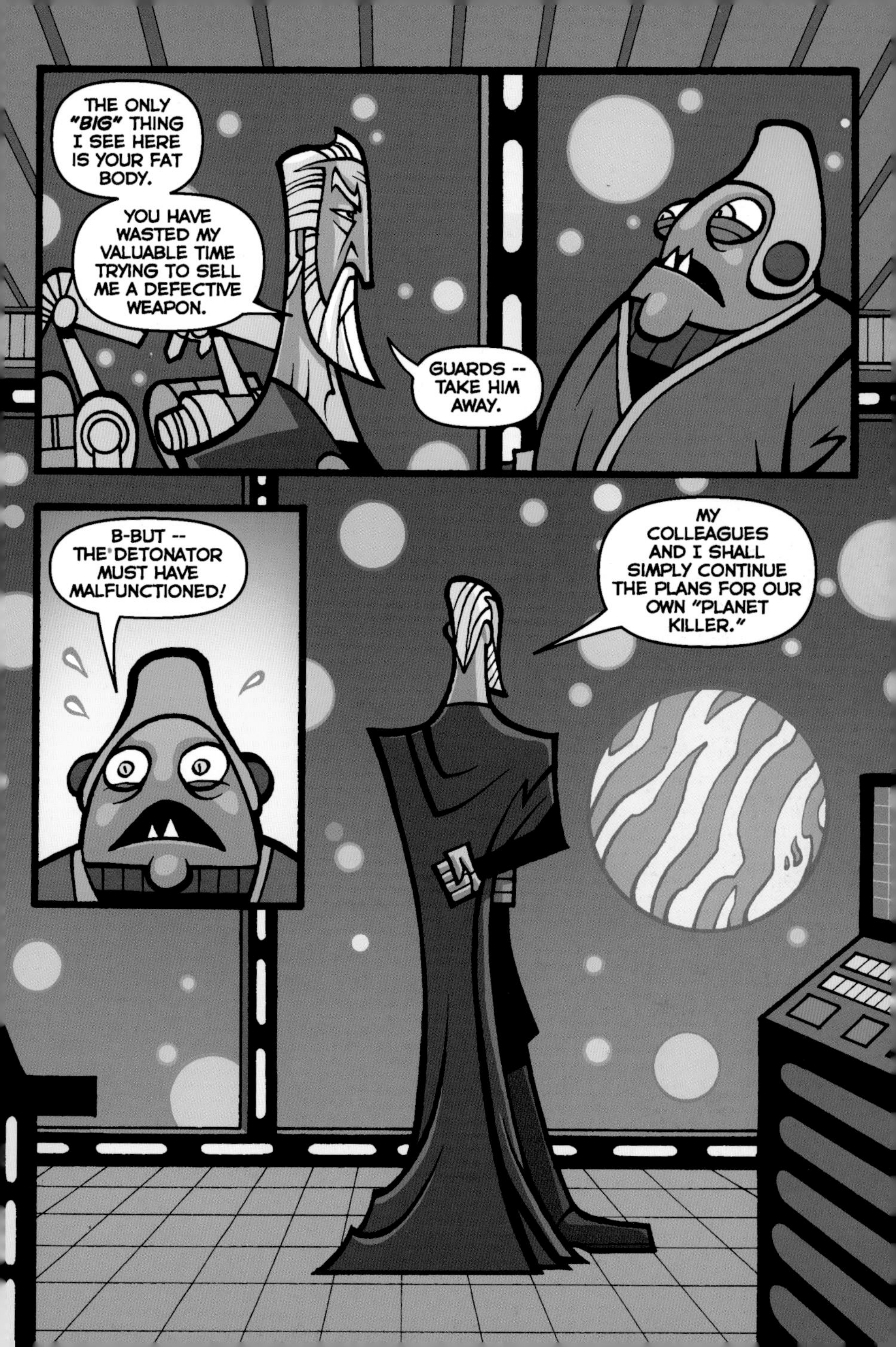
THE ONLY "BIG" THING I SEE HERE IS YOUR FAT BODY.
YOU HAVE WASTED MY VALUABLE TIME TRYING TO SELL ME A DEFECTIVE WEAPON.
GUARDS -- TAKE HIM AWAY.
B-BUT -- THE DETONATOR MUST HAVE MALFUNCTIONED!
MY COLLEAGUES AND I SHALL SIMPLY CONTINUE THE PLANS FOR OUR OWN "PLANET KILLER."

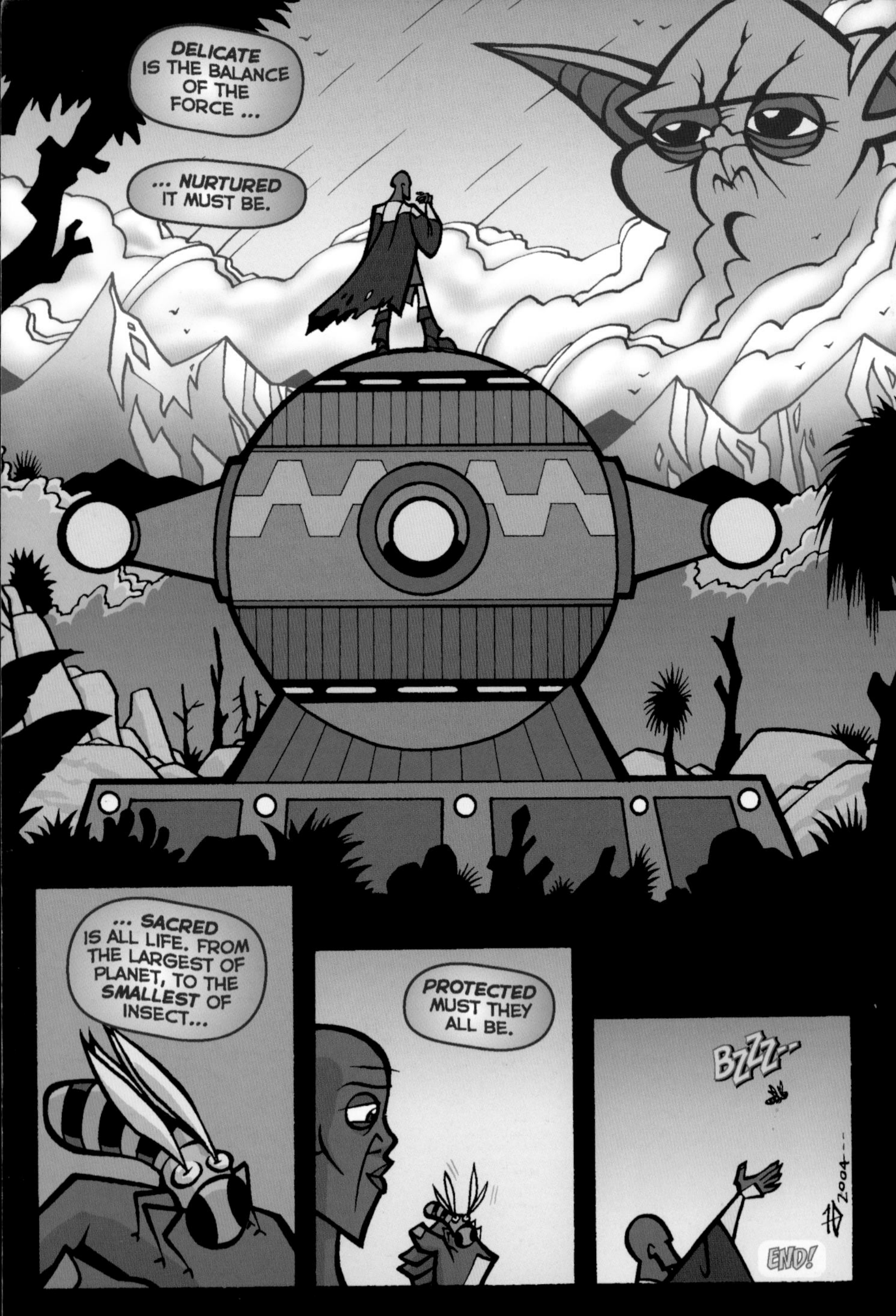
DELICATE IS THE BALANCE OF THE FORCE ...
... NURTURED IT MUST BE.
... SACRED IS ALL LIFE. FROM THE LARGEST OF PLANET, TO THE SMALLEST OF INSECT...
PROTECTED MUST THEY ALL BE.
BZZZ--
2004
END!

TIMELINE OF TRADE PAPERBACKS AND GRAPHIC NOVELS!

Old Republic Era:
25,000-1000 years before Star Wars: A New Hope

Tales of the Jedi
Knights of the Old Republic
ISBN: 1-56971-020-1 $14.95

Dark Lords of the Sith
ISBN: 1-56971-095-3 $17.95

The Sith War
ISBN: 1-56971-173-9 $17.95

The Golden Age of the Sith
ISBN: 1-56971-229-8 $16.95

The Freedon Nadd Uprising
ISBN: 1-56971-307-3 $5.95

The Fall of the Sith Empire
ISBN: 1-56971-320-0 $15.95

Redemption
ISBN: 1-56971-535-1 $14.95

Jedi vs. Sith
ISBN: 1-56971-649-8 $17.95

Rise of the Empire Era:
1000-0 years before Star Wars: A New Hope

The Stark Hyperspace War
ISBN: 1-56971-985-3 $12.95

Prelude to Rebellion
ISBN: 1-56971-448-7 $14.95

Jedi Council
Acts of War
ISBN: 1-56971-539-4 $12.95

Darth Maul
ISBN: 1-56971-542-4 $12.95

Jedi Council
Emissaries to Malastare
ISBN: 1-56971-545-9 $15.95

Episode I - The Phantom Menace
ISBN: 1-56971-359-6 $12.95

Episode I - The Phantom Menace Adventures
ISBN: 1-56971-443-6 $12.95

Episode I - The Phantom Menace - Manga #1 (of 2)
ISBN: 1-56971-483-5 $9.95

Episode I - The Phantom Menace - Manga #2 (of 2)
ISBN: 1-56971-484-3 $9.95

Outlander
ISBN: 1-56971-514-9 $14.95

Star Wars: Jango Fett -- Open Seasons
ISBN: 1-56971-671-4 $12.95

The Bounty Hunters
ISBN: 1-56971-467-3 $12.95

Twilight
ISBN: 1-56971-558-0 $12.95

The Hunt for Aurra Sing
ISBN: 1-56971-651-X $12.95

Darkness
ISBN: 1-56971-659-5 $12.95

The Rite of Passage
ISBN: 1-59307-042-X $12.95

Zam Wesell GN
ISBN: 1-56971-624-2 $5.95

Jango Fett GN
ISBN: 1-56971-650-1 $5.95

Episode II -- Attack of the Clones
ISBN: 1-56971-609-9 $17.95

Clone Wars Volume 1:
The Defense of Kamino
ISBN: 1-56971-962-4 $14.95

Clone Wars Volume 2: Victories and Sacrifices
ISBN: 1-56971-969-1 $14.95

Clone Wars Adventures Vol. 1
ISBN: 1-59307-243-0 $6.95

Clone Wars Volume 3: Last Stand on Jabiim
ISBN: 1-59307-006-3 $14.95

Clone Wars Volume 4: Light and Dark
ISBN: 1-59307-195-7 $16.95

Droids - The Kalarba Adventures
ISBN: 1-56971-064-3 $17.95

Droids - Rebellion
ISBN: 1-56971-224-7 $14.95

Classic Star Wars - Han Solo At Stars' End
ISBN: 1-56971-254-9 $6.95

Boba Fett - Enemy of The Empire
ISBN: 1-56971-407-X $12.95

Dark Forces - Soldier for the Empire GSA
ISBN: 1-56971-348-0 $14.95

Mara Jade - By the Emperor's Hand
ISBN: 1-56971-401-0 $15.95

Underworld
ISBN: 1-56971-618-8 $15.95

Empire Vol. 1: Betrayal
ISBN: 1-56971-964-0 $12.95

Empire Vol. 2: Darklighter
ISBN: 1-56971-975-6 $17.95

Rebellion Era:
0-5 years after Star Wars: A New Hope

A New Hope - Manga #1 (of 4)
ISBN: 1-56971-362-6 $9.95

A New Hope - Manga #2 (of 4)
ISBN: 1-56971-363-4 $9.95

A New Hope - Manga #3 (of 4)
ISBN: 1-56971-364-2 $9.95

A New Hope - Manga #4 (of 4)
ISBN: 1-56971-365-0 $9.95

Classic Star Wars, Vol. 1: In Deadly Pursuit
ISBN: 1-56971-109-7 $16.95

Classic Star Wars, Vol. 2: The Rebel Storm
ISBN: 1-56971-106-2 $16.95

Classic Star Wars, Vol. 3: Escape to Hoth
ISBN: 1-56971-093-7 $16.95

Classic Star Wars - The Early Adventures
ISBN: 1-56971-178-X $19.95

Jabba the Hutt - The Art of the Deal
ISBN: 1-56971-310-3 $9.95

Vader's Quest
ISBN: 1-56971-415-0 $11.95

Splinter of the Mind's Eye
ISBN: 1-56971-223-9 $14.95

A Long Time Ago... Volume 1: Doomworld
ISBN: 1-56971-754-0 $29.95

A Long Time Ago... Volume 2:
Dark Encounters
ISBN: 1-56971-785-0 $29.95

A Long Time Ago...
Volume 3: Resurrection of Evil
ISBN: 1-56971-786-9 $29.95

A Long Time Ago... Volume 4:
Screams in the Void
ISBN: 1-56971-787-7 $29.95

TIMELINE OF TRADE PAPERBACKS AND GRAPHIC NOVELS!

A Long Time Ago... Volume 5: Fool's Bounty
ISBN: 1-56971-906-3 $29.

A Long Time Ago...
Volume 6: Wookiee World
ISBN: 1-56971-907-1 $29.95

A Long Time Ago...
Volume 7: Far, Far Away
ISBN: 1-56971-908-X $29.95

Battle of the Bounty Hunters
Pop-Up Book
ISBN: 1-56971-129-1 $17.95

Shadows of the Empire
ISBN: 1-56971-183-6 $17.95

The Empire Strikes Back -
The Special Edition
ISBN: 1-56971-234-4 $9.95

The Empire Strikes Back - Manga #1 (of 4)
ISBN: 1-56971-390-1 $9.95

The Empire Strikes Back - Manga #2 (of 4)
ISBN: 1-56971-391-X $9.95

The Empire Strikes Back - Manga #3 (of 4)
ISBN: 1-56971-392-8 $9.95

The Empire Strikes Back - Manga #4 (of 4)
ISBN: 1-56971-393-6 $9.95

Return of the Jedi -
The Special Edition
ISBN: 1-56971-235-2 $9.95

Return of the Jedi - Manga #1 (of 4)
ISBN: 1-56971-394-4 $9.95

Return of the Jedi - Manga #2 (of 4)
ISBN: 1-56971-395-2 $9.95

Return of the Jedi - Manga #3 (of 4)
ISBN: 1-56971-396-0 $9.95

Return of the Jedi - Manga #4 (of 4)
ISBN: 1-56971-397-9 $9.95

New Republic Era:
5-25 years after
Star Wars: A New Hope

X-Wing
Rouge Squadron
The Phantom Affair
ISBN: 1-56971-251-4 $12.95

Battleground Tatooine
ISBN: 1-56971-276-X $12.95

The Warrior Princess
ISBN: 1-56971-330-8 $12.95

Requiem for a Rogue
ISBN: 1-56971-331-6 $12.95

In the Empire's Service
ISBN: 1-56971-383-9$12.95

Blood and Honor
ISBN: 1-56971-387-1 $12.95

Masquerade
ISBN: 1-56971-487-8 $12.95

Mandatory Retirement
ISBN: 1-56971-492-4$12.95

Shadows of the Empire
Evolution
ISBN: 1-56971-441-X $14.95

Dark Forces
Rebel Agent
ISBN: 1-56971-400-2 $14.95

Jedi Knight
ISBN: 1-56971-433-9 $14.95

Heir to the Empire
ISBN: 1-56971-202-6 $19.95

Dark Force Rising
ISBN: 1-56971-269-7 $17.95

The Last Command
ISBN: 1-56971-378-2 $17.95

Dark Empire II
ISBN: 1-56971-119-4 $17.95

Dark Empire
3rd Edition
ISBN: 1-59307-039-X $16.95

Empire's End
ISBN: 1-56971-306-5 $5.95

Boba Fett: Death, Lies, & Treachery
ISBN: 1-56971-311-1 $12.95

Crimson Empire
ISBN: 1-56971-355-3 $17.95

Crimson Empire II
Council of Blood
ISBN: 1-56971-410-X $17.95

Jedi Academy
Leviathan
ISBN: 1-56971-456-8 $11.95

Union
ISBN: 1-56971-464-9 $12.95

New Jedi Order Era:
25+ yeas after Star Wars: A New Hope

Chewbacca
ISBN: 1-56971-515-7 $12.95

Infinities:
Does not apply to timeline

Infinities - A New Hope
ISBN: 1-56971-648-X $12.95

Infinities -
Return of the Jedi
ISBN: 1-59307-206-6 $12.95

Infinities -
The Empire Strikes Back
ISBN: 1-56971-904-7 $12.95

Star Wars Tales Volume 1
ISBN: 1-56971-619-6 $19.95

Star Wars Tales Volume 2
ISBN: 1-56971-757-5 $19.95

Star Wars Tales Volume 3
ISBN: 1-56971-836-9 $19.95

Star Wars Tales Volume 4
ISBN: 1-56971-989-6 $19.95